Write Masterful Fiction

The Complete Course on Planning and Writing Stories that Publishers Love

Russel Brownlee

ARCTURI PRESS

Cape Town

Arcturi Press
Cape Town
www.russelbrownlee.com

Write Masterful Fiction: The Complete Course on Planning and Writing Stories that Publishers Love– 1st ed.
ISBN 978-0-620-93581-4

Contents

Start Writing Masterful Fiction

You've got a longing to write, a dream of creating works that move and inspire people or which change lives by imparting the wisdom of your hard-won experience. Perhaps you have flashes of insights, moments when the words pour out of you and you get the feeling this is going to be so easy. But then the inspiration dries up and you're left staring at the blank page.

Or perhaps you've made serious inroads on a story and you've got pages and pages piling up, but you know the writing itself isn't as electrifying as it needs to be. Maybe you've had some crushing feedback saying the dialogue is wooden or the story is going nowhere or you're doing too much telling and not enough showing.

That can hurt. I've been there and I must confess I sometimes still go there. The truth is that writing is an ongoing journey of learning and experience and we're never done. But here's the good news – there are just a few core skills that form the basis of all great writing. If you make a start at learning these then I can guarantee you'll be streets ahead of most beginner writers out there who are just winging it and hoping to end up with a masterpiece.

I know this because in my work as an editor and author coach I get tons of stories to assess and mostly I end up having to break the news to writers that their work just isn't ready for publishing. Their ideas might be brilliant, their dreams and ambitions might be soaring high, but the text on the page just doesn't get lift-off. And it's not just me ranting about these fatal errors, it's publishers and agents too. This is what they all complain about:

- Weak openings
- Rambling events and incoherent story structure
- Lousy pacing (too fast or too slow)
- Stock characters with no depth or inner conflict
- Wooden or clichéd dialogue
- Telling rather than showing
- Cringe-worthy descriptions and overdone prose

And those are just some of the issues. When I saw these problems in manuscripts, I began referring authors to writing how-to manuals and courses. As the list of my referrals grew longer, I began to wish I had just one place to send them that would teach them everything they needed to know. But there wasn't, so there was only one thing left to do – I created it myself.

This book is your complete, all-in-one, basic-to-intermediate fiction writing course. We're going to cover those fatal flaws I told you about and then we'll take it even further and answer those other questions you've also probably got:

- What point of view should I write in ('I' or 'he/she')?
- What tense should I write in (past or present)?
- How do I deal with the blank page and write when I don't know what to write about?
- And how do I put everything together in the form of scenes and a simple plot structure?

All these questions will be answered so you really will have everything you need to write a publishable short story or collection of scenes that can go into a longer work like a novel, memoir or screenplay.

Will this book work for memoir and creative nonfiction?

While this book is aimed at writers of fiction, it also offers the perfect fundamental skills curriculum for authors working on crossover forms such as memoir and creative nonfiction. All the skills used in structuring and writing fiction are directly applicable to true-life stories, histories, personal essays and any other form that uses the techniques of fiction to tell a story based on real life. Where necessary, the chapters have specific sections dealing with the application of the principles to nonfiction. This course can be your launchpad to exploring those other forms in more detail later.

Structure of the book

This book is the full-text version of a video course that is available on Udemy and other learning platforms, which is why I refer to it both as a book and a course. Each chapter covers one of the core skills and understandings that you'll need as a writer of fiction. Some of the lessons are about writing skills and some are about story generation and structure. Together, these will help you develop both the framework as well as the content for your stories.

At the end of each chapter, you'll find exercises that will reinforce what you've just learned and help you create your own story. We'll build narratives from the ground up and layer on more scenes as we go. If you've already started a story or even a novel or memoir, don't worry – everything you learn here will deepen what you're already doing and will bring you new ideas for characters, scenes and events.

While the chapters build upon each other in the form of a step-by-step story-building course, they are also quite self-contained, so you can also just pick out the chapters that are most relevant for you as you encounter challenges and questions in your writing.

The book covers the two essential elements of fiction writing – story structure and writing technique – in three parts:

Part 1 begins with an introduction to freewriting where you'll learn how to get words onto the page even when you don't know what to write about. Then we begin looking at structure and you'll see how stories are created from just a few basic elements. Here you'll experiment with possible story ideas and premises to work on as you progress with the course. You'll also see how to create compelling fictional characters and you'll brainstorm some characters for your own stories.

In Part 2 we shift to writing techniques and cover essential skills such as writing authentic dialogue, creating vivid descriptions and making sure you do more 'showing' than 'telling'. We'll keep building on the story ideas and characters from Part 1 as we layer on more skills.

In Part 3 we return to story structure and you'll see how to expand a story premise into a complete plot with an arresting beginning, a suspenseful middle and a satisfying end. The highlight of this part is the Story Generator – a tool that will help you map out your story and show you what you need to write next to bring it to completion.

Part 4 is a bonus set of chapters on living the writing life, setting goals, developing the right attitude and taking the next steps towards publishing. I'll answer common questions on publishing models, when to get edited and what level of editing you might need.

When you finish this course, you will have all the knowledge you need to write masterful prose that captivates agents and publishers as well as your reading public. Let's get writing!

PART 1

Story beginnings

Everybody knows what a story is until they have to sit down and write one. In this section, you will find out how stories work and you will explore ideas for building your own story. By the end of Part 1, you will have at least one story idea or premise that you can continue working on through the rest of the course.

CHAPTER 1

Getting the Words Flowing with Freewriting

Here we are at the start of a challenging and inspiring journey into the world of story and creative writing. This course is about the techniques of great writing as well as the structure of stories and the mechanics of story generation. But before we even start thinking about writing well and creating stories that work we need something even more basic – a flow of words onto the page. In this chapter I will introduce you to freewriting as the fundamental practice for all your writing sessions. It's the ultimate antidote to writer's block and the key to accessing the deeper parts of your creative mind.

As a new writer, or even as an experienced writer, you will almost certainly have experienced the delight of writing in a state of flow, where the words just appear effortlessly, or where the ideas for stories and characters just well up from somewhere deep within. It's moments like these that get us all fired up to become writers or artists. Now I don't know about you, but what often happens with me is that I sit down brimming with energy and enthusiasm, write and write for a few pages, and then everything just stops. Or I arrive at the page, expecting to continue from where I was yesterday, and suddenly there's nothing there. Not a word. Not an idea. Nada. Just me with the blank page.

If there's one thing that connects all writers throughout history it's probably that moment when the blank page utterly defeats their creative intentions and remains implacably blank. I once heard a novelist refer to it as the 50-page demon because her initial inspiration always seemed to be good for the first 50 pages of a book. But after that, the blank page lay in wait for her, and then the real work began.

The truth is that a writer is not a person who is always in a state of flow and inspiration. A writer is a person who has the courage and patience to push on through when the page fights back and swallows all their words.

Opening the channel to your creative mind

My sure-fire technique to counter the blank page is the practice of freewriting. Freewriting involves writing with no purpose and no concern for what emerges onto the page. You scrap all rules of grammar, good writing, plotting, and any intention to get somewhere and simply allow words to fall onto the page or your word-processing document in whatever order they appear. You write even though you have nothing to say. You just write, filling the page with nonsense or with lines and lines of petty complaint – whatever enters your mind, you just put it down in words. This is your free area to break away from the confines of 'good writing' and give a voice to the other aspects of your Self that want to be expressed.

I first took up the practice of freewriting many years ago when I read Julia Cameron's book *The Artist's Way*. Her practice of morning pages is an application of freewriting that has become popular with writers, and for very good reason. She advocates the discipline of doing three pages of freewriting every morning before you start any actual writing. I must admit that I don't use it in that way, but where it has become invaluable is in those times when I simply don't know what to write and I feel blocked. That's when I sit down and I start filling pages with words. I don't care what they say; I just get it all out there.

Sometimes what is revealed through this writing is that I am angry or bothered about something, and this just wells up and I find myself writing the most petty, horrible stuff. I am tempted to judge it, but then I remind myself that this is freewriting and I am dialoguing with my inner being, not writing anything for publishing. And so I continue writing until it's all out and there really is nothing more to be said on it. I am often left in a calm and inwardly focused state, the ideal condition for hearing the soft calling of the Muse and her words of inspiration.

Freewriting works by restoring flow in two areas – your mind and your energy field.

1. Restoring mental flow through freewriting

One of the main causes of the blank-page syndrome is a mental self-consciousness about what we are writing. As some of the initial inspiration wears off, we get hit by a bunch of fears or concerns, like:

- It's not good enough.
- I don't know what happens next.
- I'm feeling angry or sad.
- I have to get this right.

When this happens, we need to take the pressure off trying to write purposefully and write about what is most real for us in this moment. I call it giving expression to what wants to be said. What wants to be said is often very different from what you think you should say. What wants to be said might be something like this:

> I'm supposed to be writing this damn short story but
> I'm bored with it, it's silly, why did I even start it, maybe
> we should trash it now and start again. But then I'll feel
> a failure, I already feel a failure, it's true I am a failure,
> damn, this is pathetic ... and doing this freewriting
> thing is really so much blah, I don't even believe in it, it's
> all a waste of time, I should just go back to bed, but
> that's so boring! And now there's a bird looking at me
> through the window. Tweet, tweet.

In examples like the one above, what wants to be expressed is the voice of the shadow self, the one who has been put to one side so that more purposeful writing can happen. Sometimes you will encounter the voice of the inner child who doesn't want to do any adult writing and just wants to mess about. You have to let these voices be expressed because they exist as an energy within you that needs to be honoured and heard. Freewriting is the pressure valve that lets this energy be released.

And here's the real beauty of this setup – when we do listen to these voices, they always have a gift for us. When they have spoken the words that want to be said, you arrive at a place of calm that reconnects you with your power and creativity *at a deeper level than before.* You sit down to write, thinking that you are meant to do the next chapter, but perhaps what you are meant to do is work through the argument you had with a friend so that you can contact what you are really feeling inside. You might be avoiding your anger or hurt, but when you connect with these emotions through your freewriting, you find that they contain the energy for the next phase of your artistic creation.

The blank page is not necessarily a block – it is an invitation to reconnect with something in you that you might have been avoiding so that you can reclaim your power and authenticity. All you have to do is sit down and write.

2. Restoring energy flow through freewriting

So far I've spoken about freewriting as a way of expressing what wants to be said and getting flow happening at a psychological level. However, there is another huge benefit to freewriting, and this has to do with the physical flow of energy that happens when you write.

Getting stuck on a blank page means the writing energy is frozen. It will tend to continue in this frozen state until something powerful happens to free it. This could be the arrival of some new inspiration, but one can wait a long time for that to happen. A much quicker way to get the writing energy flowing is simply to start flowing with writing – even if what you are writing is apparently nonsense.

When you are physically moving your hand across the page or keyboard and allowing what wants to be said to appear, the energy is flowing. And this flow of energy will lead you to a more artistic expression of what wants to be said. In other words, it will lead to the finding of true inspiration. If you just sit staring at the page, castigating yourself for not being able to write, the energy is getting all bunched up and jangled, and you're rapidly falling out of love with your writing. Simply stop with the stopping, and get your hands moving. Write about the weather, about your inability to write, about the silly thing your cat is doing. Just write. And as you do this, you'll notice your energy shifts and you'll be in the flow again.

I can summarise everything I've just said about freewriting and getting the writing flowing when you don't know what to write about with this simple formula:

When you encounter the blank page, don't let the page be blank.

That's all it is. Simply sit down in front of the blank page or screen and start filling it up with words. Any words. Sooner or later they will carry you to something surprising. Freewriting gets you out of your conscious mind and what it thinks you should write about and delivers you into the inspiration zone where you are surprised by what shows up. Freewriting is writing *into* the unknown, and the unknown is the place where the adventures happen.

How to do freewriting

The basic instruction for doing freewriting is simple: Write continuously without thought or preparation and with no goal in mind other than to express your in-the-moment impressions and insights. Pay absolutely no heed to grammar or any rules of good writing and disregard any attempts to make the writing mean anything or get anywhere. Just write.

Easy enough, you might say, but it's surprising how challenging the practice can be. Here are some tips and guidelines that will help you get the most from it:

- Keep writing until you hit gold or you fill three A4 (foolscap) pages. This means, write without thinking until something usable appears. If nothing appears, continue without pause until you've written three pages. Three pages is generally the minimum to get past your mind's resistance to doing this exercise.
- Try writing with paper and pen as it can be more tactile than typing on a keyboard.
- Let the writing be absolutely uninhibited. It's not going to be seen by anyone else, so give yourself the freedom to follow your train of thought wherever it leads.
- Allow yourself to be petty, vindictive, vengeful, angry, sad, bored, frustrated, rude – all those emotional states you don't want to feel but which are in you anyway.
- If you don't know where to start, write about exactly what you notice in the moment. Start with the sights and sounds around you, your emotional state, your hopes, fears and dreams.
- Do not stop and think. Do not compose. Write into the unknown.
- Be open to unexpected statements, lines of dialogue or story ideas that just appear on the page as if by magic. When that happens, follow the thread and explore what's just emerged.

Do freewriting every day as a writing discipline or use it only when you're stuck. If you find yourself sitting and staring at a blank page for more than a few minutes, put your writing ambitions aside for a moment and just do freewriting. Something is trying to get your attention, and the freewriting will give it the chance to express itself.

Two ways to use freewriting

Use freewriting when a) you have absolutely no clue what to write about, and b) when you want to explore a particular idea or scene but can't yet find the words for it.

a) When you have no clue what to write about

This is when you arrive at your desk feeling absolutely stumped. You don't have any story ideas or you feel the story you've been telling has run out of steam. This is when you open up your A4 jotter or a blank Word document and commit to writing three pages nonstop and without thought. Just write about the weather and how stumped you are. Do this until three pages are full, then come back the next day and see if you have any ideas. If not, do three more pages. Carry on like this until you strike gold. Be patient – it can sometimes take days. But when you do hit the vein of inspiration, it will be at a new level of expression. Sometimes, your truly authentic writing voice only emerges after days of plumbing the void. So when you have dark days, just sit and do your practice and the practice will carry you to the other side.

b) To explore an idea or scene

Quite often you'll have a good idea of what should happen next in your story but for some reason the words are just not flowing. For example, suppose you have to write a dialogue between Joe and Melissa that ends in an argument. However, you're not exactly sure what they're going to argue about or even what leads up to the argument. So right now, as a demonstration, I'm going to do some freewriting on Joe and Melissa and see where it leads. I'm going to start with an utterly lame greeting and then I'll take it from there:

> 'Hi Joe,' says Melissa, 'how are you?'
>
> 'I'm fine thanks,' replies Joe. 'How are you?'
>
> 'Also fine. Just bored with this conversation. It doesn't go anywhere.'
>
> 'Kind of like our life, I guess,' says Joe.
>
> 'What's that supposed to mean?'
>
> 'Well it's the truth, isn't it? I mean, we're hanging out together and that's nice, but ... I don't know ... I just want something more.'
>
> 'Do you mean ... get married? Oh, Joseph!'
>
> 'Um, more like ... get more space. Do you know what I mean? I'm sorry.'

I didn't know where that was going to go but it certainly got somewhere fast. You can see where the story started to kick in when Melissa said she was bored with the conversation and Joe followed by expressing his own dissatisfaction. I really had no idea that was going to happen and it just emerged naturally from the totally lame beginning. Now if I really was writing a story with Joe and Melissa I would consider whether this direction took me where I wanted to go. If it did, I'd develop it further. If not, I'd start another free-writing conversation. At some point, somebody is going to say something that surprises us all.

In all the exercises you'll do in this course I'll remind you to do some freewriting on the subject if you don't have any immediate ideas. The main thing to remember is to never sit staring at the blank page. There's only one rule, after all:

When you encounter the blank page, don't let the page be blank.

Your writing practice

If you are going to make progress at your writing you are going to need to develop a regular writing practice. You need to write every day, not just once or twice a week when you don't have other things to do. Think of your writing as if it's a person you're in love with. When you're in love with someone you think about them all the time and you can't wait to see them again. You steal time from other things. You move heaven and earth to bring yourself closer to them. You don't relegate them to a Sunday afternoon when you've got nothing else to do. The truth is that if you want to fulfil your writing dream you're going to have to fall in love with your art and you're going to have to make sacrifices for it.

The first commitment is simply to start creating a routine that includes at least 45 minutes writing time every day. If you need to steal time from something else, do it. If you need to speak to someone to get some uninterrupted sacred space, do it. Decide that writing matters and that you're willing to take the risk of exploring it. There are absolutely no guarantees about any outcome. You might be wasting your time by the standards of society. But you are doing the work of your soul which is longing for a challenge that enables it to express itself. So at least for the duration of this course, take a chance and begin shaping your day so that it can include time for your art. Time for you.

When you have created the regular times, then pitch up to them and sit there with your computer or your notebook and start writing. If you don't know what to write, do freewriting. If all you do is freewrite three pages, then you've done your writing work for the session. The only thing that matters is that you honour your writing time and that you fill it with writing or with planning your stories. By this regular practice you are creating the vessel that your inspiration will fill with content. It takes work and commitment to build the vessel, but once your inner mind starts to trust that you are always going to show up for your dates and that you are taking this thing seriously it will start showing up for the dates as well. But *you* have got to show up first.

The context of this lesson

I've put this lesson right up front because freewriting is your number-one practice to get the words and ideas flowing. Freewriting frees you from having to try to think up stories when you have no ideas. It takes you beyond your ordinary mind and into the world of true inspiration. Do freewriting for all the exercises in this course the moment you feel stuck or empty of ideas.

Summary

The main ideas from this chapter:
- Freewriting is uncomposed, uncensored writing that stops you over-thinking and takes you into the inspiration zone.
- Whenever you are faced with the blank page, don't let it be blank. Fill it up with words and see where they take you.
- Freewriting breaks through psychological blocks as well as energy blocks.
- It is important that you develop a regular writing practice and to stick to it. Regularity trains the unconscious mind to deliver story ideas in a steady stream. If you don't know what to write about in your session, just freewrite until something interesting happens.

Exercises

1. Develop a writing practice

Decide on a time of day you are going to keep sacred for your writing. If you have to make any arrangements or speak to anyone to get this free time, do it. Tell your partner or anyone you live with that this is important and that you hope to have their support in this. Then pitch up to the practice. Give yourself a few days to adjust and to find the best writing times. It can help to have two possible times so if one is disrupted you can still make it to the second one. PS ... you can do the exercises in this course during your daily practice sessions. Each chapter's exercises should take you two to three sessions (45–60 minutes each), so every three to five days you can start a new chapter. By the end of this course your writing practice will be firmly in place.

Note your writing times in a diary or notebook and commit to them. For example, *I write every weekday at 7 AM or 6 PM for at least 45 minutes, and every Saturday and Sunday at 8 AM for at least 60 minutes.*

2. Freewrite three pages

At least once, try freewriting with no idea what to write about. Write until three pages are filled. If you've got more to say after three pages, carry on going. Notice how your energy shifts as you write – you might find the words start slowly then flow fast, or they may slow to an absolute trickle and even stop at a point. If that happens, don't start thinking about what to write, just listen inwardly and begin writing or typing again. It might feel a bit uncomfortable because you are going beyond your mind and entering unfamiliar territory. Do this exercise at least once. Do it every day if you arrive at your writing space and don't know what to write about.

3. Freewrite on a theme

Choose any one of the following story prompts and freewrite on it for a few paragraphs. See if it goes anywhere.

- While walking in the park you see something unusual or disturbing.
- A woman spills coffee on a man at a coffee shop.
- A waitress at a diner is having a bad day.
- A child makes an unusual request.
- A beggar or stranger asks you for something.
- You receive a strange message from an unknown number (or an out-of-character message from someone you know).
- Someone stops you in the street and says something that unnerves you.

CHAPTER 2

The Four Modes of Writing

Think about what we do when we write a story. We narrate a series of events, we describe settings and characters, and we help the reader understand things by providing explanations. Narration, description and explanation. These are actually three of the four classic modes of discourse identified way back in ancient Greece. Now you may be wondering why I'm giving a history lesson here, but just stay with me a while and it will all become clear. Knowing about the modes of writing and when to use them provides you with a key to diagnose problems in your text and to write with more power and vibrancy.

Here is an outline of the four modes of discourse (or the four modes of writing) with some examples of each:

- Narration: Writing that conveys a story to an audience. It focuses on putting events into a sequence, which is essentially what storytelling is all about – a series of events. Narration includes specific techniques through which the author tells their story, for example, point of view, tense, voice, narrative structure (plotting) and most of the things we'll be covering in this course. Narration examples: Biography, memoir, novel, oral history, short story.

- Description: Writing that creates a sensory experience for the reader and allows them to fully picture and imagine the setting and characters. Description examples: Journal writing, poetry.

- Exposition: Writing that aims to explain and inform. It may also include description if the description gives the reader necessary information rather than just poetic or sensory detail. Exposition is used in fiction to present backstories and facts that the reader needs to know. Exposition examples: Business letters, articles, scientific reports, textbooks, academic essays.

- Argumentation/persuasion: Writing that aims to prove a point or argue a position. This mode should generally be avoided in fiction as any form of overt persuasion in a story is probably going to alienate readers. Fiction readers want to feel something, not be told something. Argumentation examples: Critical essays, reviews, advertising copy.

You can get combinations of these modes in any piece of writing. For instance, *narrative exposition* in a story is where you give background information about the setting, characters or past events. It's used when you quickly want to tell the reader some important information before getting on with the story. Most of the exposition in a short story or novel usually happens somewhere near the beginning, but there might also be shorter passages throughout the text.

As this course focuses on the writing of fiction or creative nonfiction (rather than poetry or essays) we'll focus on the techniques of narration while also touching on description and exposition. They all have a part to play in your creative writing – the secret is just in getting the balance right for your particular writing project.

The context of this lesson

Knowing about the four types of writing gives us a vocabulary and set of tools to begin to analyse our own writing and to diagnose any problems that might arise. For instance, suppose you've written a story (narration) and you've received some feedback that says the pace is a bit slow and there are a few boring passages with no dialogue or action. If a story is coming across as boring or slow there's a good chance it's because you're doing a bit too much explaining (exposition) or describing (description). Too much exposition can make your story start reading like an essay, while a lot of description can sound wonderfully poetic but it puts your readers to sleep.

Summary

Key points from this chapter:
- There are four classic modes of discourse (types of writing): narrative, description, exposition, argumentation.
- Knowing the appropriate mode of discourse for your writing project can help you communicate more effec-

tively and help you diagnose any problems with the writing.

- The dominant mode in fiction is narration, with smaller amounts of description and exposition.

Exercises

There are no formal exercises for this lesson. However, next time you read any news articles, textbooks or fiction, begin noticing what modes of discourse are being used. Especially with fiction, see if you can find instances where you think the author is doing too much explaining or describing, or perhaps not doing enough. This will help you begin to get a sense of the four modes of writing and when each one is used appropriately.

CHAPTER 3

Finding Your Story Idea

In this chapter we'll start the story-creation process by unpacking the basic mechanics of storytelling. You'll see how stories are created from just a few basic elements and you'll experiment with possible story ideas to work on as you progress with the course.

The art of telling stories really boils down to one thing – the ability to evoke curiosity in the reader. Your job is to make people curious enough so they'll read the first page and then the next and the next. While some people seem to have an innate ability to tell stories, when it comes to the written word there is a lot that simply comes down to technique and knowing the basics of engaging writing. You will be able to generate curiosity in the reader when you begin to build aspects of writing like these into your work:

- A story that moves at just the right pace, in other words it is well structured.

- Engaging characters who evoke an emotional response in the reader.
- Sparkling dialogue that drives the story and contains unexpected twists and turns.
- Vivid description that creates a sense of movement and of things about to happen.
- Evoked emotion through showing character reactions rather than telling readers what to feel.
- And most of all, creating ongoing conflict that compels the reader to carry on reading so they can find out how the conflict is resolved.

In this course we'll be covering all of these points, and we're going to begin with the most fundamental one – conflict.

Disruption of the ordinary world

Even though we writers are generally peace-loving animals, our trade is in conflict and disharmony. If this sounds a bit odd, just think about your life when everything is going well and you have no setbacks or conflicts at all. Things are just rosy. Now the question is – would you be able to write a fascinating and engaging story about your rosy, happy life?

I'm willing to bet that if you actually sat down to plot your story you wouldn't get very far. When everything is happy and perfect then nothing really matters because nothing can be lost. There's absolutely zero drama. Story only happens when that happy life is threatened. In other words, story happens when conflict arrives and disrupts the existing order (known in story terms as the 'ordinary world'), creating a situation of lack or need. The lack drives action to resolve the lack, and that's where the proper story begins.

Never mistake a series of events for a story. If there's no conflict that links those events in matrix of lack-desire-action, then nothing is really happening. Events don't make a story. Needs and desires do. Readers read stories so they can experience the thrill of losing something and then finding it, or finding something different that's even better. They read because they want the delicious feeling that happens whenever a conflict is resolved. It's chemical. Like a sugar-rush.

So what, exactly, is conflict in narration? Conflict arises when something or someone causes a disruption in a character's life that causes them to want something. This conflict can be dramatic or extremely subtle. And it can be internal or external, and preferably both.

There are six common types of conflict in stories: man versus self, man versus man, man versus society, man versus nature, man versus fate (or gods/supernatural) and man versus technology. It's important to note that 'man' stands for 'human' and is not specific to any gender. Stories usually contain more than one kind of conflict.

Conflict 1: Man versus self

These are the internal battles that a character wages within themselves. Man vs self is the only internal conflict type – all the others are external. Man vs self will occur in most stories, though it might not be the dominant conflict. In a man-vs-self conflict, for example, someone might battle an addiction or be tempted to go against their values in order to get something they need. Whenever someone faces mixed emotions about something, they are experiencing a man-vs-self conflict.

Man-vs-self conflicts are often the dominant conflicts in works of a more literary nature where the psychological growth or decline of a character is the main focus. Stories that have very little man-vs-self conflict can come across as quite shallow.

Conflict 2: Man versus man

This is when your hero (the protagonist) faces off against another person (the antagonist). It's your classic hero vs opponent conflict. But it doesn't have to be that dramatic and can also involve a more subtle conflict between, say, a group of friends. A love story is also a type of man vs man conflict. The lovers seek each other while something keeps them apart. They may even fight and appear to hate each other until they reconcile their inner conflicts and get together at the end.

Conflict 3: Man versus society

This is an external conflict that involves a protagonist at odds with a ruling body or the norms and values of a social group. In this type of conflict, the social group will usually be represented by one or several people who act as the antagonists. For example, if a woman is facing the judgements of a conservative church she might stand off against the preacher and one or two congregants. This means the man vs society conflict is also a man vs man conflict.

Conflict 4: Man versus nature

This conflict pits humans against deadly animals or natural forces such as tornadoes, floods, volcanoes, asteroids and plagues.

Conflict 5: Man versus fate

The protagonist finds himself or herself at the mercy of a capricious or vengeful god, a supernatural force or blind fate. A central theme might involve the necessity of coming to terms with one's humanity or physical limitations. This is one kind of conflict the protagonist is often set up to lose so they can win some kind of understanding or undergo a change of attitude (i.e., the man-vs-fate conflict forces them into a man-vs-self conflict). For example:

- Romeo and Juliet as 'star-crossed' lovers.
- Two teenagers battling cancer fall in love.
- A man loses his family and all his money and must start a new life.

Conflict 6: Man versus technology

The protagonist faces a challenge from machines or technology. This is a conflict often found in science fiction. The man-vs-technology conflict will often also involve a man-vs-society conflict as the technology might belong to another culture or might even form its own culture. Think of the Cylons in *Battlestar Galactica*.

If you are wondering where comedy fits into all of this talk on conflict, then the answer is it fits everywhere. Conflict gives rise to comedy just as easily as it gives rise to drama and tragedy. A man slipping on a banana skin is pure conflict in action (man vs fate/nature).

How conflict gives rise to stories

Conflict disrupts the status quo or state of balance in a character's life, bringing them either something they don't want or taking away something they do want. This creates a *desire* to remedy the situation, leading to *action*, which creates *more conflict* and gives rise to the story quest.

You can also think of conflict simply as the problem. A character in a particular situation has a problem which they desire to solve or avoid.

In the classic works on plotting and story structure, conflict/problem arises when a character's ordinary world is disrupted by an inciting event. We can express it like this:

- A character
- in a situation (ordinary world)
- encounters a problem (disruption and conflict).

For instance, suppose a stay-at-home mum is looking after her baby while doing a creative writing course in her free moments. This is her ordinary world. But then one day she hears a scream from her neighbour's house and rushes to the window to see the husband leaving the house in a hurry. This is the disruption – it disrupts her ordinary world by making her a witness to a mystery. Now she will be in some kind of conflict – should she go over and see if anyone needs her help, or should she pretend she didn't see or hear anything?

Sometimes the character's ordinary world is already full of conflict and the disruption just ramps it up or takes it in a new direction. Suppose we have a character, Alice, who has finished school and really wants to go to college, but she doesn't have the money. She works as a cashier and tries selling her artwork to raise money. This is her ordinary world and it already contains conflict in the form of frustrated desire. This is almost enough for a story, but we need to ramp up the conflict a bit more or else we won't go anywhere interesting. Now suppose one day a wealthy and somewhat mysterious man takes a shine to young Alice and makes her a proposal, offering her 'one night for one year'. If she spends just one night with him, he will pay her tuition and lodging for one year. The offer is an intense disruption of her situation and compels her to act, unleashing further conflict and drama.

Another example of a story starting with an already conflict-rich ordinary world is *The Hunger Games* by Suzanne Collins. The story opens with the people of the districts eking out an existence under severe oppression at the hands of the rulers in the capital. The hero, Katniss Everdean, makes do under the circumstances and exists in a state of relative balance. But then the draw for the gladiatorial hunger games is held and her kid sister is chosen as a participant. Katniss can't let this happen, so she volunteers to go in her place. Her life, as she knows it, is over.

The story idea

The character + situation + disruption/conflict gives you your *story idea*. This is the general setup for the story – the ingredients that combine to get things moving. To describe the story idea, we can give the initial situation and character followed by words like 'but' or 'until' to indicate the disruption. Or we can begin with the word 'when'. For example:

> Joe was happily married *until* he discovered his talent for gambling.

When a tornado rips through Kansas farmland, a girl and her dog are swept away to a magical land.

You can probably see why this is called the story idea – it really is just the very first thought you might have for a story before you've properly figured out how it's going to work. Another way a story idea might come to you is when you find yourself using the word 'suppose'. As in:

Suppose a girl is forced to compete in a fight-to-the-death TV reality show set in a dystopian future world. (*The Hunger Games*)

In this *Hunger Games* example, you've got a character (a girl), a situation (a gladiatorial TV reality show in a dystopian future world) and disruption (she's forced to fight).

You get the picture – the story idea is any formulation that gives the general situation in which your story is going to unfold. Note that you also don't always need to state the ordinary world explicitly – it's usually enough to imply it in the character description or let us deduce it from the disrupting event. In the *Wizard of Oz* example, the ordinary world is a Kansas farm. That's all we really need to know at first. Or suppose you have a story where your disruption is the moment an asteroid strikes the earth. You don't need to say that all was OK with Joe's world until the day the asteroid struck. Just say, for example:

When an asteroid hits Earth, Joe Bloggs finds himself alone in a city of a million dead.

Let's have some fun with story ideas using the six classic conflicts described earlier. (See if you can spot the ones that are based on movies or TV series.)

Omar and Layla fall in love but their families have been locked in a murderous feud for a hundred years. (Man vs society, man vs man)

*

The police chief of a seaside town looks forward to a peaceful summer tourist season, but then a gigantic white shark begins eating people and nobody wants to get in the water. (Man vs nature, man vs self)

*

When a woman in a conservative society decides to leave her abusive marriage, she is cast out by her church and left with no support. (Man vs society, man vs self)

*

Young monk Athelstan has dedicated his life to God's work in the monastery of Lindisfarne, but when Vikings attack he is captured and taken back to Denmark as the slave of the warlord Ragnar Lothbrok. (Man vs fate, man vs man, man vs self)

*

Freed slaves Jim and Maria begin working an abandoned patch of land with the dream of turning it into a prosperous smallholding. All goes well until swarms of locusts arrive and a conservative preacher blames the newcomers for the arrival of the plague. (Man vs nature, man vs fate, man vs man)

*

After 20 years of peace, an old battleship used in the Cylon wars is being disarmed and decommissioned. But then the Cylons launch a surprise attack and destroy the humans' homeworld. Only the old battleship and a few other transport ships survive. (Man vs technology, man vs man)

*

A misunderstood, sci-fi addicted kid picks up a coded message on his home-made radio when he directs his antenna towards Mars. He becomes convinced the message contains plans of an alien invasion. (Man vs man, man vs self)

In the examples above there are a few that come from actual movies or TV series but the rest I made up in just a few minutes. Conflict situations are everywhere and all of them can be used to create a story.

When you define the conflict your character faces you actually create the character in the process. The conflict gives them a need or desire and this leads to choices, actions, learning and growth or the failure to grow. So conflict drives both character and action. Don't worry if this all feels a bit much at the moment – we'll touch on it again several times in the coming lessons and by the end of the course, you'll be an expert in it.

Story idea in memoir and creative nonfiction

If you're writing a memoir, biography or work of creative nonfiction that's based on true events rather than a fictional story, do you still need to think in terms of conflict and story idea?

Most definitely. Even if your subject draws from actual events and the facts of a person's life, you're still telling a story. Your job is to find the hook or angle that opens the story and keeps it unfolding in a riveting way. For instance, if you're writing a biography of someone called Marco, the worst thing you can do is start with a statement like, 'Marco was born in Naples on April 1, 1966'. Unless there's something particularly auspicious about that date, there's absolutely no story there and your reader will be tempted to put the book down. They don't want a chronology of every event from first breath to last – they want a story. That means that you need to find the moment of conflict that changes the person's life and either start with that or build up to it in a very purposeful manner.

So if you're writing a memoir, what was the real start of your adventure? What problem, challenge or event happened that compelled you to set out on a quest for a solution or which gave you the theme you want to explore? Start with that and end with the lesson being learned or the theme being explored and integrated.

The context of this lesson

The whole aim of this book and course is to get you writing publishable fiction that gets past the critical eyes of agents and publishers. And one of their big complaints is that writers don't know what their central conflicts are and don't get to them quick enough. They spend time on peripheral events when they should be focusing on setting up the core conflict that drives the story and motivates the characters. So this is your first step in creating powerful narratives that grab attention from the start and compel people to read on.

This knowledge is also important because conflict creates character and plot, and we'll be dealing with those subjects in upcoming lessons. If you know that conflict is the beginning of a story, you have the power to generate an endless supply of story ideas.

Summary

The main ideas in this chapter:
- Conflict disrupts a character's ordinary world and gives rise to desire which leads to action and the quest for resolution. This is the starting point of any story.
- There are six common types of conflict in stories: man vs self, man vs man, man vs society, man vs nature, man vs fate (or gods/supernatural) and man vs technology.
- Stories usually have more than one type of conflict.
- The story idea can be expressed as character + initial situation + disruption (conflict).

Exercises

1. Brainstorm story ideas

Brainstorm (freewrite) some story ideas. Don't think too much about it, just have fun dreaming up characters and situations. Story ideas are usually expressed in terms of a character in an initial situation plus a disruption that introduces conflict. The disruption/conflict is often introduced by the words 'but', 'until' or 'when'. Make up at least three story ideas and identify the main categories of conflict involved, for example, man vs man and man vs self. If you like, you can use the plot of a favourite book, movie or TV series for one of your options.

Example: *A young man proposes to his girlfriend but then war breaks out and he's drafted into the army. (Man vs fate, man vs man)*

2. Story idea for a story you are already working on

Do this exercise only if you are already working on a story that you would like to build on during this course.

For your existing story, who is your main character (or characters) and what is the central conflict they are facing? Express it as a story idea naming the character, their initial situation and the disruption (using 'but', 'until' or 'when', or any other suitable formulation).

Your story idea:

Formulating Your Story Premise

In the previous lesson we discussed the role of conflict and how it forms the seed of all stories. If everything is sunshine 'n roses down on the farm, there just ain't no story. But when clouds of locusts appear, that's when things get interesting.

When you did the exercise on brainstorming story ideas you would have come up with some dramatic or even comical conflicts and challenges for your character. At this point you've almost got enough to get a story going but you're still missing one thing – action. Your hero has to be launched into some kind of action as the first step to resolving their conflict. We can express this as:

- A character
- in a situation (ordinary world)
- encounters a problem (disruption and conflict)
- and must *take action* or bad things happen.

When you bundle all of this information together into a statement you have something very valuable – your *story premise*. If you read up on the definition of premise, you'll find many different answers. About the only thing that people agree on is that premise is the thing that makes your story work. It describes the essential ingredients that set everything in motion and keep it going until the satisfying end. Usually, this boils down to a character, their problem and what they have to do to start solving it. You can remember the formula with this nippy little statement:

A character has a problem and must take action or else bad things happen.

While the story idea discussed in the previous lesson outlined the basic setup of character, situation and problem, these statements can be quite general and still very much up in the world of ideas. Take this example:

> A woman in a conservative town wants to leave her abusive marriage but, if she does so, her church will cast her out and she'll be left alone with no support.

As a story idea this is great, but it really only points us in the direction of a possible story. To see if we really have a story worth writing, we need to develop this into a premise by getting really specific about the character, their problem *and* the actions they have to take.

Formulating the premise

While the conflict is usually introduced with the words 'but', 'until' or 'when', the action is introduced with words and phrases that indicate some kind of decision or forced action. For example:

- must
- has to
- forced to
- decides to
- caught up into
- finds herself/himself

These words and phrases are often preceded by the word 'now', as in: '*Now he must* find a way to blow up the Death Star and save the Rebel base.'

Here are some story ideas and premises of popular books or shows:

Barry (HBO series)

Story idea: An assassin tires of making a living by killing people and wants to go straight. But his past won't let him go.

Premise: Ex-marine-turned-assassin Barry Block tires of making a living by killing people and takes up acting classes so he can get in touch with his emotions and live a normal life. But a Chechen drug cartel has put out a hit on him and he is *forced* to defend himself in the only way he knows how.

The Hunger Games (Suzanne Collins)

Story idea: A teenage girl lives in a future world where children must fight for their lives in a brutal gladiatorial contest for the entertainment of the ruling class. *When* her little sister is chosen as a contestant in the games, she volunteers to go in her place.

Premise: *When* Katniss Everdean's little sister is chosen to be a contestant in a fight-to-the-death TV reality show, Katniss volunteers to go instead. *Now she must* prepare herself for a ruthless combat game in which life and death depend as much on fighting skill as on winning the favour of a bloodthirsty audience.

The Wizard of Oz (MGM)

Story idea: When a tornado rips through farmland, a girl and her dog are swept away to a magical land.

Premise: *When* a tornado rips through Kansas, Dorothy and her dog, Toto, are swept away to the magical land of Oz. *Now they must* go on a journey to find a wizard who can help them return home.

Let's think up some new concepts and premises. Any formulation is permissible as long as it contains character, problem and action.

A killer asteroid is heading to earth and the only person who can stop it is a washed up, drunken former astronaut with a death wish and a warrant of arrest in five states. NASA *must* convince him to get sober and save the world.

*

Brainy but lonely teenager Lincoln Mudge sits in his room every night thinking about life on other planets and the impossibility of ever finding true love. *But* one night, while looking at the moon through his binoculars, he sees the girl next door sitting at her window crying. He *decides* to investigate.

*

> Brad, a tech-loving bachelor, devotes his spare hours to creating a smart home that he can control with his phone. *But* then his fridge starts ordering beer and pornography and his TV sends him subliminal messages to go over to his neighbours with a chainsaw. *Now he must* fight to reclaim control as a malicious AI entity tries to take over his life and replicate itself to everyone in his contact list.

The important thing about the premise is not the exact wording, it's whether it sparks curiosity in the reader and makes a promise of an adventure. Even more importantly, it gives us as writers a structure to work with that will generate meaningful action and genuine character development.

Premises for short stories

The premise formula I've described is designed for full-length works of fiction like novels and screenplays. It can work for short stories as well, but the reality is that some short stories are little more than a character facing a challenge leading to some kind of climax or transformative moment (also called the *epiphany*). They often don't get as far as taking any meaningful action, so the 'now he must ...' formula doesn't always apply. If you are thinking about writing short stories, then it can be OK to stay with something simpler like the story idea (character + problem) and then add the epiphany. We'll look at short stories in more detail in the module on basic story structure.

Premises for memoirs

A memoir is a story about you. It's not your autobiography, which is your whole life, but rather the story of a particular aspect of your life or interesting time in your life. For instance, you could write a memoir about overcoming an illness or about a year spent hitchhiking around the world. Even though it's about the truth, you still have to organise that truth into a readable story, so you're going to have to make decisions about where you begin telling the story and how you end it. Most importantly, you're going to have to look for the lessons you learned or the key piece of knowledge that you want your reader to walk away with. In other words, you're going to have to get clear on what the real story is. What is the psychological, spiritual or philosophical point you wish to make and what is the story of you coming to that understanding? Think of the hugely popular *Eat, Pray, Love* by Elizabeth Gilbert. It reads kind of like a novel because it tells a properly structured story – a woman going through a breakup travels the world to find meaning. It's not just a travel story – it's also a spiritual quest and a love story.

So what does the premise for a memoir look like? As it turns out, it's very much like the premise for general fiction, except that instead of focusing on the action the hero has to take, you focus on the lesson or insight that you learned.

1. **A character:** You or someone else you're writing about.

2. **A situation:** The subject of your memoir. For instance, your year spent living as a writer in Paris or your experiences covering the war in Iraq.

3. **A lesson:** What did you learn from this experience or how did your life change as a result of it? Lessons are often introduced by the words 'discovers', 'learns', or 'finds'. Instead of a

lesson you could have a theme and arrange your narration to explore that theme in detail.

> Example: *When* a young reporter is sent to cover the Allied invasion of Iraq, she *discovers* that victory is not the end of war but merely the first step on a journey into darkness.

Troubleshooter

If you're already writing a full-length story like a novel or screenplay, does your story seem to be drifting aimlessly and are you having trouble creating an effective ending? If so, it could be because the foundation of your story is missing a key ingredient. If you don't have an interesting character with a conflict, goal and real consequences for failure, then you might just find yourself writing for years and not getting anywhere. So check to see that you have a workable premise and, if not, do some reworking of the story to bring in what's missing.

The context of this lesson

This lesson is critical because your story will need a premise as the basis of a more detailed plotting structure, which we'll cover later. Knowing how to draft story premises gives you a tool to generate new ideas for stories and to get a sense of whether they will work before you even start writing.

The other really good reason to know how to construct a premise is that agents and publishers are going to ask you up-front what your story premise is, so you've got to have it ready. No premise, no publishing.

Summary

The premise outlines the character (with initial situation), the conflict they face and the action they must take to begin setting it right.

Exercises

1. Creating story premises

Write at least three premises for new stories. You can start with some of the story ideas you created in the previous exercise and just add the action that the character needs to take. Or create some new ones.

Don't let yourself get stumped by getting the wording absolutely right. As long as you've got a character with a challenge and some kind of action you'll be fine.

Here's an example premise written in two different styles to get you started:

Version 1: Alfie Jones, a misunderstood, sci-fi addicted kid, picks up a coded message on his homemade radio *when* he directs his antenna towards Mars. He becomes convinced the message contains plans of an alien invasion and *must* persuade his sceptical parents and friends that the danger is real.

Version 2: *When* Alfie Jones, a misunderstood, sci-fi addicted kid, picks up a coded message on his homemade radio, he becomes convinced the message contains plans of an alien invasion. *Now he must* persuade his sceptical parents and friends that the danger is real.

Over to you (write at least three premises):

---

2. *Your story premise*

This exercise has two options. Do option A if you are already working on a story and option B if you haven't yet started anything.

Option A: Do this exercise if you are already writing a full-length story like a novel or memoir. Write down the premise of your story detailing character, challenge and action (or lesson/insight/theme if you're writing a memoir). If you feel your story can't fit into this structure, create your own premise statement. The only rule is that it should hook the reader and promise some kind of adventure or character development.

Option B: If you aren't yet writing a story, choose one that you created above in *Exercise 1 Creating Story Premises* that you think you might be able to work on and write it in the space below. Or create a new premise. Note: This doesn't commit you to anything and you can work on different story ideas and premises as you go through the course. The important thing is just to get some ideas flowing right now.

Your premise:

CHAPTER 5

Creating Characters

In the previous chapters we discussed the role of conflict in story creation and how it gives rise to a story idea and then a story premise. A premise is generally considered to be a short formulation of the character, the problem they face and what they need to do to solve the problem.

In this chapter we'll start layering some flesh and substance onto the basic idea or premise by creating your main characters. The characters are *who* your story is about. Readers, agents and publishers are looking for dynamic characters who struggle and who are vulnerable, who triumph but also fail. They want characters with depth and purpose. So that's what we're going to give them.

The basics of character building

Stories have major and minor characters, flat and round characters, and, of course, heroes and villains.

1. *The main players: heroes and villains*

Firstly, every story will have at least two characters – a protagonist and an antagonist. The protagonist is the main character or hero. There is usually only one protagonist, though complex stories can have more. The protagonist is the person who the story is really all about.

The antagonist is the character who opposes the protagonist. It is often the villain or 'bad guy' but could also be a force of nature, for example, a tornado, an asteroid, or a shark. It could also be the lover in a romance or romantic comedy. If Mary, the protagonist, wants James to marry her, then her conflict is with him, so he is the antagonist.

2. *Character types*

Some of your characters will be complex and undergo a process of growth or regression, while others will be there simply to perform a function of some kind. Generally, we can think of characters as being flat or round.

Flat characters are one-dimensional figures, often functional as stereotypes, for example, the spoiled child, the seductress, the tough ex-soldier, and the minion who does the bidding of the bad guy. They are usually morally unambiguous – in other words, they are clearly good, bad or neutral. Flat characters usually don't change much during the story, so they are considered to be static. They are also generally the minor characters in any story.

Round characters are fully imagined people with a range of traits, including positive and negative characteristics. They have faults as well as virtues and they have both inner and outer conflicts. Round characters usually change in some way, so they are dynamic. These are the story's major characters.

Flat characters are your supporting actors and actresses, while round characters are your stars. They're the people we bond with or become fascinated by. Think of Hannibal Lecter in *Silence of the Lambs* – we don't bond with him, but we're certainly fascinated by him. We're drawn in by some strange spell. It's probably because Hannibal is extremely complex and layered, with the horror of his cannibalism balanced by his intelligence, refinement and moral code. Hannibal is a resonant and memorable character precisely because he is at once so human and so inhuman. If he had just been presented as an evil cannibal (a flat character) the movie wouldn't have been the success it was because we simply don't care what happens to flat characters. But round, complex characters make us begin to care, because we see ourselves in them. They show us who we could be, given different circumstances.

Tip: When you create your protagonists and antagonists, let your bad guys have some good in them, and let your good guys have some bad in them (or at least a weakness). In fact, your protagonist and antagonist often mirror each other in certain ways. For example, if a cop is chasing a killer, the cop had better be good at defending herself and even capable of killing someone if she stands a chance of catching him. The cop might need to tread some murky waters where the boundaries between law and criminality, order and disorder, are blurred.

3. Character goals

All your main characters will have goals they are striving for. You'll remember from the discussion on premise that the story begins when a character is faced with a conflict and has to do something to resolve it. The conflict gives them a goal – something they either want to attain or avoid. While you might have many characters with goals, it's your protagonist's goals that create the structure of the story.

The character goals can be either external or internal. Ideally, you want your protagonist to have both external action goals and inner growth goals. The external goals are created by the external conflicts (e.g. man vs nature) and they give rise to the physical action in the story. We can refer to them as action goals. Characters are usually very clear on their action goals – they know what they have to do, even if it usually turns out to be the wrong thing at first.

The internal goals are created by the man-vs-self conflict that is sparked by the inciting event. Inner goals drive character growth and transformation. The important thing to note is that characters are usually not aware of their inner goals at first. They think all they have to do to solve their problem is satisfy their outer goals. But as the story progresses there comes a point where they have to confront their personal weaknesses and undergo a transformation of some kind. While the protagonist is usually not aware of their inner goal at first, you as the writer need to know what that is. The inner goal will come from who they are – their character, their past, their inner demons and their limiting beliefs.

Here's an example using one of the story premises created in the previous chapter.

Alfie Jones, a misunderstood, sci-fi addicted kid, picks up a coded message on his homemade radio when he di-

rects his antenna towards Mars. He becomes convinced
the message contains plans of an alien invasion and
must persuade his sceptical parents and friends that the
danger is real.

The part about Alfie persuading his sceptical parents and
friends about the danger of an alien invasion is his action goal.
It's what he has to *do*. His inner goal is not immediately apparent, but we can guess it has something to do with his character
trait of being misunderstood and addicted to science fiction.
He's probably a super brainy introvert more at home in the inner world of his imagination than in the outer world where he
has to deal with people. In order to succeed at his outer goal he
will have to change something within himself so that he can be
understood and get people to take him seriously. It's this conflict and goal that will give the story emotional depth and which
will cause the reader to bond with the character.

Weaving inner and outer goals together

The most memorable stories have characters with both an outer
desire and goal and an inner desire and goal. We speak of the
outer desire as what the character *wants*, and the inner desire as
what the character *needs*. For example, Joe might spend most of
the movie trying to get Sally as a lover, but what he really needs
is to love himself first. He can only achieve his outer goal (the
want) once he has achieved the inner goal (the need). This adds
a layer of depth to the story that is truly engaging because it
deals with universal truth. The need is usually a quality of being
that the character has lost and needs to find, for example, self-

love. Or it can be a false belief they have about themselves, for example, 'I am unworthy of true love'.

While the outer events in the story are particular to that story, the inner needs are more universal and thus engage the reader more deeply. Here are some examples of outer goals (the wants) and inner goals (the needs):

Want: To save the world and defeat evil once and for all
Need: To learn humility and wisdom

Want: To find a magical sword that will restore power to the king
Need: To find power and authority within

Want: To stay in a failing marriage
Need: To learn to draw boundaries and stand up for oneself

Think of Luke Skywalker in the very first Star Wars movie (now called *Star Wars Episode IV*). What he wants at the beginning is to live a peaceful life on his uncle's farm. But when he is drawn into the fight against Darth Vader it becomes clear that his inner need is to own his power and to be a warrior. Once he begins owning his power his outer want changes from avoidance to fully engaged action as he leads a strike against the death star and faces Darth Vader in a duel. Ultimately, this is a movie about inner growth and facing one's light and dark aspects.

Another great example of a protagonist with inner and outer goals is in the movie *Wonder Woman* (2017). You'd expect a movie like this to be all action goals without much inner change, but this movie is an exception. The writers give Wonder Woman a character development arc driven by her outer want as well as an inner need. Her want is to defeat the evil antagonist and rid the world of war forever. She has a kind of innocent pride that gives rise to wonderfully comic scenes as she tries to disguise her goddess-abilities from the general public. But when she defeats the evil antagonist at the end and achieves her action goal, she also loses the man she loves. She discovers her vulnerability, and this opens her to her deeper need, which is to be truly human. She achieves an outer victory but she is also humbled in the process. This makes her more human and, therefore, more engaging to us because now we can identify with her. She is a super-human, but she is also us. In the final scene she reflects on her new desire to work *with* people rather than trying to solve their problems for them. By giving Wonder Woman a human need, the writers deepened the story and made it memorable and transformative.

What readers and audiences sometimes think they want is action and adventure, but what they really need is an emotional release. They want to walk away feeling they have been changed in some way and that some aspect of their own nature has been seen. I call this *heart*. Books and movies with heart are irresistible because they help us feel something we've been missing.

A weak point of the action and thriller genre is that quite often there's so much action there's not much room for the inner journey of the protagonist. The writers over-rely on plot and tension to create an effect, but somehow the heart of the story goes missing. The heart is the personal wants, dreams, needs and vulnerabilities of the protagonist. Another action movie that got this right is the first of the Jason Bourne movies – *The Bourne Identity*. The film has a brilliant premise that goes something like this: A CIA agent loses his memory and doesn't know who he is. Now he must discover the truth of his identity while fighting for his life as a rogue CIA unit sends assassins to kill him.

The story is gripping because we go with Jason as he discovers mysterious things about himself – for instance, that he is an expert at weapons and defending himself. He faces external conflict in the form of assassins sent to kill him but also internal conflict as he discovers more of his true identity. It's a character mystery as much as an action movie.

Now compare this to the second and third Bourne movies (if you've seen them). They are really just long car chases punctuated by explosions. Totally forgettable. The filmmakers forgot that the success of the first movie was that it drew us into a character mystery where the car chases and explosions were secondary. It got us to care about the character as he grappled with a universal question – *who am I really?*

Your first job with your main characters is to make your readers care. And readers don't care for pure characters, whether purely evil or purely good. There's nothing as boring as a nice person who always does nice things. Your readers will care about your characters when your characters have both outer wants and inner needs, and when these wants and needs are in some kind of tension. The needs are about the character's secrets and woundedness. They are what engage recognition and feeling in the audience.

The fatal flaw

You'll hear the concept of the fatal flaw brought up quite often in writing courses. The fatal flaw is the hero's weak point. Their wound. It's the thing that needs healing. If they don't heal, the story will end as some form of tragedy.

If you're guessing that the fatal flaw is connected to the need, you'd be correct. The fatal flaw is just another way of describing the protagonist's need. It's what they really need to do if they are to achieve what they're looking for. The fatal flaw is usually a quality of being that they lack or a negative belief they have about themselves or the world. The fatal flaw is the place where the antagonist attacks them, but it's also the doorway to victory. If the protagonist heals their flaw, they will take a huge step towards victory over the antagonist.

This doesn't mean your protagonist *should* heal their flaw – it all depends on what kind of story you're writing and the effect you want to achieve. Sometimes characters will get what they want in the outer world but they won't get what they need in the inner world. This kind of ending tends to be bitter-sweet. They have achieved victory, but it has come at a cost. This very realisation can be the effect you want your audience to walk away with. Fiction isn't supposed to deliver a lesson, but you can deliver an insight or effect which amounts to a lesson of some kind. Sometimes the lesson is a dark yet truthful one about human nature. In *The Godfather* trilogy, for instance, the third movie ends where Michael Corleone has achieved every possible success as a mafia boss, but he's lost the one thing most dear to him – his family. He never healed his fatal flaw, and this creates a tragic ending that is poignant and moving.

If you give your characters an inner need or fatal flaw your possibilities for endings are far greater than if it's all about going for some kind of outer goal. With only an outer goal, all you've got is success or failure. Either he wins or he loses. But if you add an inner goal, then you can have combinations and effects like these:

- Outer success achieved through inner success creates a sense of triumph.
- Outer success with inner failure is tragic or bittersweet.
- Inner success with outer failure creates a sense of resigned wisdom.
- Inner failure and outer failure is abject tragedy.

The antagonist's ray of light

If the protagonist has a fatal flaw, the antagonist should have a ray of light – something that makes them human and possibly redeemable. Of course, not all the antagonists you find in literature and the movies have redeemable features, but the most memorable ones do. Every antagonist is a hero in his or her own story. Everyone thinks they're doing good, even if they have to do terrible things to achieve it.

Think of Michael Corleone of *The Godfather*. At the beginning of the story, he is determined to stay out of the family business and live a law-abiding life. But when his father is shot it awakens his prime value – defending his family at all costs. This is inherently good – we can all respect the desire to defend our families. It's just that in Michael's case it takes him on a journey so deeply into darkness that he ends up losing his family. The point is that if he were just an evil man we would not have stuck with the story through three long movies. Something engaged us, and that had to do with his desire to protect what he loved.

In *Star Wars: The Return of the Jedi*, the evil antagonist, Darth Vader, is redeemed when he saves his son, Luke, and is mortally wounded in the process. Subsequent episodes in the saga reveal

Darth Vader's backstory and how he was seduced by the dark side of the Force. However, he retained that original goodness – the ray of light, which enabled his final redemption.

Do you absolutely have to have a rounded, redeemable antagonist? The quick answer is no. Just be wary of making your antagonist unbelievably evil or cruel as you might end up creating a character that is so flat and unrealistic that the audience fails to engage with the story as a whole. I've seen manuscripts where the bad guy just rants and raves the whole time and you end up switching off and not caring anymore. Why? Because they're just not realistic, and if the enemy is not real, then what is the hero going to fight against? The more real you make your antagonist, the more real the hero will have to be – and that makes for engaging writing.

Tip: Experiment with the notion of giving your bad guy a human side – something that makes them redeemable, or at least understandable.

Building your characters

Round characters are built on two levels – the outer and the inner. The outer layer is their appearance, gender, age and any quirks or observable things that make them unique. It's also about their external goal. The inner layer is about their personality and the psychological needs and contradictions that create inner conflict in their lives. This gives them their inner goals.

The outer layer

When you get an idea for a story you might also get a sense of how your characters look and behave. It's a good idea to write all this down because in doing so you might discover new traits and get more clarity on who they are. Naturally, your flat characters will have a lot less detail than your round characters. So, for the first level of character-building, you can make notes about things like these:

- Age, race, gender.
- Appearance.
- Any special quirks or habits that make them unique, for example, walking with a limp, always moving quickly/slowly, using particular expressions and phrases.
- Their way of 'being' in the world, for example, secretive, quiet, extrovert/introvert, loud, bossy, shy, authoritarian, submissive.
- Their role or status: mother, prince, poor girl, student, middle-aged man.

The outer layer is home to the character's action goal, so you'll also want to identify that here.

The inner layer

Here you outline the character's psychology, paying special attention to their weak point and fatal flaw. This gives the need and their inner goal. In your character outline you can note any quirks, habits or elements of backstory that contribute to the inner conflict that will develop.

Let's try this on the Alfie Jones example. I've made quick notes on the premise and both the outer and inner layers of this character:

Premise: Alfie Jones, a misunderstood, sci-fi addicted kid, picks up a coded message on his home-made radio when he directs his antenna towards Mars. He becomes convinced the message contains plans of an alien invasion and must persuade his sceptical parents and friends that the danger is real.

Protagonist name: Alfie Jones

Age: 14

Appearance: Blond, freckles, wears glasses, hair messy, perhaps slightly chubby with a rare but infectious smile.

Character notes: Introvert, studious, messes about with chemistry sets and electronics in his room. Has two friends (a girl and a boy) who are equally nerdy. He has a crush on the girl but is too timid to do anything about it.

Action goals (wants): Convince friends and parents that the radio messages are from aliens wanting to invade earth.

Fatal flaw: Seeks approval from others. His worst fear is ridicule (because he is bullied for his nerdy nature and social awkwardness).

Inner goals (needs): Build self-confidence and stand his ground as people doubt and ridicule him. Learn to stand up for the truth. Gain courage. Find his voice.

That's quite a rough outline but it gives enough information to get a story going.

Creating your characters

If you're just starting out with writing then much of this information about inner and outer goals might just be a bit more than you need. We don't usually sit down to purposely create a character with well-defined wants and needs – we are more likely to be surprised by a character as they walk, slink or glide into our awareness from wherever characters are born. The work of defining their appearance, outer goals and inner needs often comes after our first hit of inspiration or our first sketches of dimly sensed characters. Sometimes, figures just show up and we have no clue what they're about to do until they do something. Or sometimes a character appears and then just drifts out again and goes off in search of another story. The main point is that characters kind of appear by themselves, and then your job as a writer is to flesh them out and discover their true role in your story.

Character building in short stories

As mentioned in the previous chapter on premise, short stories don't always have fully worked out premises. And this means they don't always have fully fleshed out characters with fatal flaws and inner needs. The aim of short stories is usually to present just a single scene or a handful of scenes that builds to some kind of surprise for the reader. So your characters are going to be like sketches – roughly drawn and unrefined. They are only there to show one aspect of human nature or to dramatise a single theme.

So if you are mainly writing short stories at the moment, don't feel pressured to make your characters fully rounded with inner needs that are eventually resolved. Short-story characters often do have an inner and outer quest, but there's no time in the story for both of these quests to be worked out. Part of the allure of the short story is that it ends abruptly, leaving things unanswered.

If you see yourself mainly as a short-story writer, do all the exercises in this module because they will make you a better writer and they will give you insight into the mechanics and the psychology of storytelling. And who knows, maybe one of your short-story characters will surprise you one day and want to become the protagonist of a longer narrative.

Character building in memoir

In a memoir, the main character is you. This means you have to start looking at yourself as a character and get clear on what strengths and weaknesses played out over the period of your life you are recounting. For instance, if you're writing a memoir of your time in a war zone, what was the personal weakness, fear, mistaken belief or challenge that you had to overcome to survive? Make the story of overcoming this weakness an organising principle of the narration, just as you would do for a fictional character. What was the moment you overcame the weakness? How did you do it? What happened as a result of this victory? Or if it was a defeat, what did you learn?

The same goes for if you are writing a biography. In this case, you are not writing about yourself but about another person. Even though it's an actual person, your work is to find the stories within the events that happened. Real people develop and grow or regress in the same way fictional characters do – they are driven by outer goals and inner needs. So do a character outline of your subject and find their goals and needs. Then tell the story of how these were resolved or left unsatisfied.

Troubleshooter

Are you already well into a story but having difficulty knowing what next to write next? Or does your story seem to have lots of action but it feels like it's not really going anywhere? Check to see whether your protagonist is truly a round character with an essential weakness that drives them to seek wholeness. A floundering story is often the result of a character who just doesn't have anything meaningful to do. They might have lots to do as far as action goes, but they have no inner conflict that gives rise to a passionate quest. Remember that the key driver of story is conflict and the search for wholeness or balance. So give your hero a real flaw that creates conflict and vulnerability in them and see how this deepens your work and generates meaningful actions.

And if your hero does have a flaw and has a path of growth, can you say the same of your antagonist? A worthy hero must have a worthy foe.

The context of this lesson

Agents, publishers and readers want characters who they care about and identify with – so as an author you need to know how to create characters who are complex, conflicted and vulnerable, just like real people. Knowing how to create authentic characters with real needs and drives is also essential from the point of view of story structure because your character's goals shape the plot. We can't discuss plot and structure if you don't know what your characters really want.

Summary

Key points from this chapter:
- Stories have flat characters and round characters. Flat characters are static and stereotyped while round charac-

ters are dynamic and have both positive and negative qualities. Stories need both flat and round characters.

- Memorable stories have protagonists who are fully rounded characters with both positive and negative characteristics.
- Round protagonists have an external want that drives action and an inner need that drives psychological growth.
- The need is also sometimes called the fatal flaw. It's the crack in the protagonist's armour that they need to address if they want to succeed at their action goal. The action journey forces them to confront their flaw and to grow.
- The protagonist can fail to learn and to heal their flaw, in which case the story has a tragic or bitter-sweet ending.

Exercises

1. Create a character

Take any character from the story ideas or premises you cooked up in the previous exercises or make up a new character just for this exercise. Give them the following:

- Appearance (appearance, quirks, defining features, name etc).
- An external goal or want (what they want to achieve through action in the world).
- An inner need (what they really need in order to be happy or to succeed at the external goal).

You can be as detailed or as brief as you like. Use the Character Outline Worksheet below to fill in the details. As always, don't let yourself get stuck on any question. Regard this as a rough draft and give yourself the liberty to play. Freewrite if necessary.

Character Outline Worksheet

1. Idea or premise for the story in which this character plays a significant role: _____
2. Character name: _____
3. Appearance: _____
4. Behaviours, quirks and mannerisms: _____
5. Personality (happy, melancholic, serious, light-hearted, surly, miserly, generous, timid, etc.): _____
6. Round characterisation (If your character is essentially good, what are their weaknesses? Or if your character is the antagonist, what are their good qualities or strengths?): _____
7. External goal/quest (want): What do they want to achieve through their actions? _____
8. Inner goal (need) or fatal flaw: What inner quality do they need to own or what belief do they need to change in order to achieve their outer goal? _____

2. A character in your work-in-progress

Do this if you are already working on a full-length story like a novel or screenplay. Take either your protagonist or antagonist and fill in the Character Outline Worksheet given in the previous exercise.

PART 2

Writing technique

The previous chapters focused on the initial planning phase of writing a story, and in this part, we shift to actual writing techniques. We'll keep building on the story ideas and characters from the previous chapters as we get to grips with the essential skills of fiction writing.

CHAPTER 6

Writing Dynamic Dialogue

Fiction is all about creating the experience of real-life through made-up stories and characters. It creates an illusion of reality that your readers will happily inhabit for a few hours or days. And because so much of what happens in reality happens as dialogue, it's no wonder that dialogue is a defining feature of fiction writing and the narrative mode. While some non-fiction also uses dialogue, it's limited to what actual people were heard to say or were recorded as saying. Non-fiction can contain pieces of dialogue, whereas in fiction it's a major feature that helps to drive the story forward.

Imagine picking up a novel and seeing that the first few pages are just paragraph after paragraph of ordinary text with nary a smidgin of the spoken word. You'd probably put it down. The fact is that dialogue not only creates a sense of realness or immediacy, it also brings spaciousness into the text and increases the reading pace. Readers want dialogue, so we need to give it to them in generous doses. The challenge for us as writers, though, is that dialogue is really easy to mess up. You can write a clumsy description and get away with it, but clumsy dialogue just sounds, well, clunky and unrealistic. It breaks the fictive spell, the illusion of reality we are working so hard to create.

The first principle to understand is that written dialogue is not real speech – it's a *representation* of real speech. Nobody really speaks like they do in written dialogue, because in real dialogue people do annoying things like:

- Hum and hah
- Mishear and ask for clarification
- Say random things that don't mean anything
- Say things in 30 words that could be said in ten

Your readers simply don't want to waste time reading all this fluff, so your job is to cut it out.

On the other hand ... you can go to the other extreme with your dialogue and create something that is so pure and perfect it comes across as wooden and sterile. You'll break the fictive spell. The trick with dialogue is to get a feel for just how much of real speech patterns to include to create the impression of reality without overloading the text and boring the reader.

Here are some aspects of real speech that you will need to bring into written speech to create more natural dialogue include:

- Beginning *in medias res*: People don't always start a dialogue at the logical beginning – they often just say stuff that comes unfiltered from their thoughts. In other words, they begin in the midst of a thought or action.

- Redirected questions: People don't always answer the questions that are put to them. They can ignore, redirect or purposely misinterpret questions. Sometimes they say nothing.
- Sentence fragments: People don't always speak in nice, grammatical sentences. They'll often just speak in phrases and sentence fragments or just say a single word.
- Interruptions: People interrupt other speakers or finish their sentences for them. Dialogue is not always a nice, even back and forth of measured responses – it can be a cut and thrust duel to the death!
- Freudian slips: People don't always have great control over what they say. They reveal aspects of themselves through things they say without intending to. Or they say inappropriate things that reveal aspects of their real character.
- Body language and meta-language: People don't only communicate with the words they use – they communicate with silences, pauses, body language, etc. Silence can speak volumes. So can a shrug or a nervous laugh.

So, in short, you want to cut out all meaningless quirks from your speech and include only those words, gestures and actions that contain meaning that's important to advance your story or deepen character. You'll create the effect of freewheeling speech, but behind the scenes you've controlled everything quite carefully. This doesn't exclude the fact that a lot of the times your characters will actually surprise you by what they say and will take the conversation in their own direction, but you still get to keep control over how that speech is presented.

You'll let them go wild and then you'll fine-tune the dialogue later.

Guidelines for great dialogue

These guidelines and principles will help you understand how dialogue works and what pitfalls to avoid when writing your character interactions.

1. Dialogue is for narration, not exposition

In Chapter 2, I introduced the modes of writing, and you might recall that narration is writing that tells a story, while exposition is about explaining things. You can have exposition in fiction (narrative exposition) where the narrator explains something about the other characters, the setting or the backstory. However, an important point to get here is that exposition is addressed to the *reader*. Dialogue, on the other hand, is a conversation between two or more characters *within* the story. Your characters should talk only to each other and not to the reader. If you put exposition in dialogue, it just sounds false.

Take a look at this example and see if you can spot what's wrong with it:

"Hi, Alex."

"Nice to see you again, Molly."

"What have you been up to?"

"Well, Molly, as you know, I'm a car salesman. I'm twenty-six years old. I've lived here in Dullsville for twelve years. I was married, but that ended last year and now I'm very lonely. I come to this bar often but so far have failed to meet anyone I particularly like."

Apart from the wooden, stilted awfulness of it, can you see how the author is using Alex's words to tell us, the reader, about his situation? Alex isn't speaking to Molly, he's speaking to us. That's why it sounds so unrealistic.

This point is essentially about showing vs telling. The example above is all 'telling'. As writers, we should rather ask how we can 'show' readers he's lonely by his actions or by the things he says without saying outright that he's lonely. For instance, he could just let slip that he's divorced and comes to the bar every day. That will show us a lot about him without ever telling us directly what his situation is.

Using dialogue to speak to the reader rather than to the other characters is essentially exposition framed by quotation marks. If you need to explain something to the reader, do this in explanatory exposition text or give it indirectly through the words of other characters. For instance, we could get Molly to let us know Alex is no longer in a relationship:

Molly took a long sip of her Martini, then said, "I heard you and Jill, you know ..."

I shrugged. "Yeah. Splitsville."

"Sorry."

"It's for the best, anyway," I said. "If you love something, let it go, or something like that ..."

"Or hunt it down and kill it."

"You're funny, Moll. It's what I always liked about you."

I think that reads a bit better. The conversation is a bit more alive and natural, and it casually drops in the information that Alex likes Molly. By the way, a tell-tale sign of an author using dialogue for exposition is when they use the phrase 'as you know'. If the character being spoken to already knows it, why say it?

"Well, Molly, *as you know*, I'm a car salesman..."

That just sounds fake. It's a dead giveaway that the author is speaking to the reader rather than to the character. Start looking for examples of this in mass-appeal commercial fiction and you'll find them.

2. Dialogue is a form of conflict

You've heard me going on and on about conflict being the starting point for a story. So it should come as no surprise when I say that conflict is the driving force of all engaging dialogue. Remember, conflict isn't always about fighting and aggression, it's present whenever someone wants something or is confronted with a truth they'd rather not face. Desire is conflict – the conflict between a full future and an empty present. Confusion is also conflict (the clash between what is known and what is unknown). The same goes for doubt, envy, greed, loneliness and just about every other human emotional experience. Even the care of a parent for a child could be laced with the conflict of fear for their safety or fear of rejection.

The key point to get here is that your dialogue should have a defined purpose that drives your story forward or deepens character – and as such it will need to be laced with conflict. A dialogue without overt or subtle conflict is boring to the reader and a waste of good paper. Let's call in Molly and Alex again:

"Hi, Alex."

"Nice to see you again, Molly."

"What have you been up to?"

"Well, Molly, as you know, I'm a car salesman. I'm twenty-six years old. I've lived here in Dullsville for twelve years. I was married, but that ended last year and now I'm very lonely. I come to this bar often but so far have failed to meet anyone I particularly like."

Is this conversation boring as hell? Yes. Is there any conflict in it? No. Not a bit. It's just mouths opening and closing, saying nothing.

Now let's look at that rewrite we did for it in the previous section:

Molly took a long sip of her Martini, then said, "I heard you and Jill, you know …"

I shrugged. "Yeah. Splitsville."

"Sorry."

"It's for the best, anyway," I said. "If you love something, let it go, or something like that …"

"Or hunt it down and kill it."

"You're funny, Moll. It's what I always liked about you."

Is that more interesting to read? Yes, I think so. Is there conflict in it? Certainly. There's the conflict of Jill and Alex splitting up. The conflict of Molly being cautious to say it out loud. Alex's conflict over losing Jill and trying to cover it up with a cliché (if you love something, let it go). Molly's edgy comment about hunting it down and killing it. And even Alex's admission that he always liked Molly has the potential for conflict. Is he still attracted to her? Will she also reject him? Is he attracted to Molly while still holding a candle for Jill? There's a lot going on in this short exchange.

Tip: If you find your dialogue is limp and lacklustre, check to see whether it's got conflict in it. If not, scrap it and start again.

3. Have a real conversation, not a ping-pong match

A ping-pong conversation is one that bounces neatly back and forth between each speaker just like a ping-pong (table tennis) game. Everyone speaks quite formally using nice, complete sentences, usually about nothing of importance at all. Just like Alex and Molly:

> "Hi, Alex."
>
> "Nice to see you again, Molly."
>
> "What have you been up to?"
>
> "Oh, I'm a car salesman. And I got divorced last year. How about you?"
>
> "I was a schoolteacher. And then I married George, a rich businessman."

Ping ... pong, back and forth. Real people just don't talk like that. They use silence and body language to communicate. They interrupt each other or get interrupted by other people or events. They start talking about something else altogether. They reply with grunts, shrugs, single words, or sentence fragments. One person might say a lot more than the other. No nice pings and pongs.

Let's see if we can bring some realness to Alex and Molly.

"Oh my goodness ... it's you. Alex Morton."

The attractive blonde I'd noticed at the bar a moment ago was now looking at me. She moved closer and recognition dawned. Molly Kohl. From high school. Plain little Moll had certainly blossomed. I just nodded and gave a goofy grin.

"What on earth are you doing here?" she said. "You were in Dullsville on your way to becoming town mayor or senator, or something."

I laughed. "Still in Dullsville, but not the mayor." I caught the barman's eye and gestured to Molly. "A drink? For old times?"

Her face clouded and she gave the barman an anxious glance. "Oh, I shouldn't," she said. "It's, well, I'm working."

"You're working. Now? Here?"

"It's a long story, OK. Maybe another time ..."

"Like when? Tomorrow?"

She gave a sad smile. "No, Alex. I'm sorry. I shouldn't have said anything. Just forget you saw me, all right? I wasn't here at all."

I think that's better. I didn't know where the conversation was going to go when I started freewriting it but it turned in an interesting direction. Are you curious about what work Molly is doing? Me too.

4. Don't start with hello!

"Hi, Alex."

"Hi, Molly. How are you?"

"I'm fine thanks. What are you up to?"

"Well, I'm a car salesman and I got divorced last year and ..."

Do yourself a favour – just nix all that 'hello, how are you?' nonsense. People are very seldom this formal in real life, so why should your characters be? Also, it's nonessential information that doesn't drive the story forward, show character, or develop conflict. If you really have to have characters greet, find a more constructive way of doing it that cuts out the formality and ping-pong. If one character has to say hi, let the other character retort in an unexpected way.

"Mornin' boy."

"Mornin' ol' man. Looks like them beeves got out in the night."

"While you were sleepin'. You'd think a young buck with good ears woulda heard it."

"Well, I had company."

"Probably why them beeves hit out for the hills. Couldn't stand all that gruntin' an' groanin'. Damn near sent me runnin' for it."

This piece begins with a greeting but it doesn't get stuck there. The second speaker redirects the greeting to the fact that the cattle have absconded from the corral, thus moving the story forward.

The anatomy of brilliant dialogue

A piece of dialogue consists of three things:
- The words spoken
- The attribution, which tells us who is speaking
- The action that occurs while characters are speaking

1. The words spoken

I'm sure you know this already – the words spoken are the bits between the quotation marks. Simple as that. We've covered most of this in the section on principles and guidelines above. And we'll cover the 'how to' of punctuating dialogue in the punctuation section later in this chapter.

2. Dialogue attribution (tags)

Attribution is what lets us know who is speaking. It's usually indicated using dialogue tags – the little phrases outside of quotation marks that name or identify the speaker. In the example below, the tags are in italics:

> "Look at yourself, Alex," *she said.* "You've become a sad and sorry loser."
>
> "No I haven't," *said Alex.*

Attribution can come after the dialogue (as in the above examples) or before it. When attribution precedes the direct speech, use a comma or a colon before the opening quote mark:

> She said, "You've made a big mistake, buddy!"

> He glared at her: "You have absolutely no idea who you're talking to."

For more on whether to use commas or colons, or when to capitalise the first word of a passage of speech, see the upcoming section on punctuation.

Attribution mistake #1: Over-using tags

The general rule is that you only need tags when it's not clear who is speaking. So don't feel you have to use tags to identify the speaker in every line of dialogue. For instance, in the example above, we could easily delete the phrase 'said Alex defensively' and the reader would still know exactly who is speaking.

On the other hand, there are instances where the reader will know who is speaking but the dialogue just sounds better with a tag. A well-placed tag can help create pace and rhythm in dialogue.

Attribution mistake #2: Getting overly creative with tag verbs

"What the hell are you up to?" he yelled.

"Nothing," she simpered.

"Well, it's ridiculous!" he expostulated.

The general advice is to stick with 'said' or 'says'. It's simple and doesn't draw attention to itself, so it almost becomes invisible. The phrasing of the character's statement will usually be enough to convey a sense of the character's emotional state while speaking, so you don't need to use descriptive verbs like 'simpered', 'exclaimed' or 'moaned'.

The exception to this is when you want to say something about the tone of the address that isn't already implied by the words the character speaks. For instance, in the first example above, the question, "What the hell are you up to?" could be spoken in several different ways, including angrily, softly, loudly, or menacingly. So in this case, it can help to clarify how the statement was uttered:

"What the hell are you up to?" he *yelled*.

Note that you do not need to say 'asked' after a question, unless you want to. It's perfectly OK to write:

"Are we going to your mother's for Christmas this year?" she *said*.

In summary, use 'said' or 'says' for everything, except where you need to clarify how a phrase was spoken because it's not already clear from the wording or punctuation.

Attribution mistake #3: Committing impossible speech acts

"Now I've got you," he *chortled*.

"No, you haven't," she *laughed*.

"Pah," he *snorted*. "You haven't got a chance."

Get this – you can't chortle, laugh, snort, sigh, growl or simper words. It's just not possible. So don't do it in your dialogue. What you can do is separate the physical description from the speech act, using a comma if you need to:

"Now I've got you," he said, then gave a gloating laugh.

"No you haven't," she said, smiling wickedly.

"This will be the end of you," he said, before breaking into a menacing laugh.

3. Dialogue action (Beats)

A dialogue beat is a short statement that describes the physical action a character performs while speaking, before speaking, or after speaking. Like a dialogue tag, it can act as a form of attribution identifying the speaker, though it is usually longer and doesn't contain the word 'said' or 'says'.

In the passage below, the bits in italics are beats:

The woman at the bar *looked up from her martini and a flicker of recognition crossed her face.* "Oh, my goodness ... it's you ... Alex Morton."

Alex turned towards her. "Ah ... Molly? Molly Kohl?" Plain little Moll had certainly blossomed since high school, he thought.

"Yes, it's me. What on earth are you doing here?" *She slid her drink along the counter and moved closer.* "You were in Dullsville on your way to becoming town mayor or senator, or something."

Alex gave a short laugh. "Still in Dullsville, but not the mayor. Not yet, anyway..."

"That's all right," she said, *dipping a finger into the martini glass and fishing out the olive.* "Mayors are old and bald, generally speaking. You can do better." *She held the olive to her mouth and bit slowly through it.* A drop of gin glistened on her lips. "This is the best part. The drunken bit at the end. Don't you think?"

See how the beats stand in for some of the tags. The reader assumes that the action being described applies to the person in the same paragraph.

Beats can stand on their own or they can be attached to attribution tags to suggest simultaneous action:

"Beats are useful parts of dialogue," he said, prodding at the blackboard with a chalky finger.

Beats serve to texture, enliven, pace and deepen the meaning of dialogue. Try bringing them into your dialogue sketches now and see how they elevate your writing to a new level of mastery.

Tip: Find your own method for adding beats. Some writers find that the beats come to them as they're writing the dialogue, while others prefer to get all the words down first and then go back and add the beats later.

Punctuating dialogue

You've written some sparkling dialogue, so now it's time to punctuate it. In this section, we'll go through some of the main rules of dialogue formatting and punctuation.

1. New speaker, new line

Each new speaker starts on a new line after a paragraph break:

"What are you doing here?" she asked.

"I'm waiting for the bus; can't you see?"

"It seems a bit of a strange place to wait for a bus." She was about to drive off when she turned and said, "Can I give you a lift?"

2. Multiple paragraphs of dialogue by the same speaker

Open each new paragraph with a quotation mark but don't close any of them until the very last paragraph.

> "I'm going to keep on talking until you really get it. Blah de blah.
>> "This is a new paragraph and I'm still not done.
>> "It's still me talking but it's midnight so I'll stop."

3. Final punctuation marks

If commas, full stops (periods), exclamation marks, question marks or anything else comes at the end of a passage of direct speech, they go *inside* the quotation marks, not outside it.

> "All final punctuation goes inside the quotation marks," he said.
>> "Are you sure about that?" she said.

4. Single vs double quotation marks

> "Should I use double quotation marks like this," he said, 'or single quotation marks like this?'

The choice comes down to whether you are writing in American English or UK and rest-of-the-world English. Americans prefer the double quote while speakers of real English (ouch!) prefer single quotes. In the end, it doesn't matter too much which you choose as long as you are consistent.

If you want to nest quotes (a quote within a quote), use single quotes if your main text uses double, and vice versa:

thing in the wording or tone of the greeting that conveys important information.

• A piece of dialogue consists of three things: the words spoken, the attribution tags telling us who is speaking, and the action that occurs while characters are speaking (dialogue beats).

Exercises

1. Write a dialogue

Write at least one page of dialogue using the correct formatting and punctuation (to the best of your ability). It can be a single dialogue or several separate dialogues (i.e., different characters and situations), so long as you fill a whole page. Don't forget to add some dialogue beats to show action. If you need help coming up with ideas for dialogues, try these writing prompts:

• A woman tells her lover she's pregnant.
• A warrior is nervous before a battle.
• Someone knocks on a door and makes a strange request or delivers troubling news.
• Two strangers share a moment of intimacy in a stuck lift (or on a bus, etc).
• A detective and a colleague discuss a crime scene.
• A child reveals a family secret to an adult.

Tip: Don't over-plan your dialogues. Just start with a vague idea, then freewrite and let your characters surprise you with what they say.

2. Dialogue from your work-in-progress

Do option A if you are already working on a story or option B if you haven't started or haven't gotten very far.

Option A: Choose a piece of dialogue from your work-in-progress that you feel could do with some improvement. Update it using the knowledge you gained in this lesson. Apply the correct punctuation to the best of your ability.

Option B: Write a dialogue involving one of your characters from the previous chapter on character development. Or a dialogue with a new character from one of the story ideas you are working with on this course.

CHAPTER 7

Choosing Your Narrative Tense

When sitting down to write a piece, one needs to decide on two major issues – the tense (past/present/future) and the point of view (first/second/third person). These can often be quite tough decisions because they are going to determine the whole feel and effect of the piece you're writing. In this chapter, we'll go through the essential elements of tense so you see what happens when we tell a story from different vantage points in time. In the next chapter, we'll look at point of view.

Past, present, future

Your scenes will take place either in the grammatical past, present, or future. The tense is indicated by the form of the verbs you use, for example, find/found, run/ran, see/saw, says/said, laughs/laughed. Take a look at these examples:

Present

I find myself running blindly. What if she catches up with me?

He asks, "What's the matter?" She doesn't answer him.

Past

I found myself running blindly. What if she caught up with me?

He asked, "What's the matter?" She didn't answer him.

Future

I will find myself running blindly. What if she catches up with me?

He will ask, "What's the matter?" She won't answer him.

You can probably see from these examples that past and present both work quite well as narrative tenses, but the future tense just sounds a bit odd. To write in future tense you have to use the word 'will' all the time, and that starts to sound strange after a while. The reality is that future tense is hardly ever used in fiction, so we can safely put it aside. But that still leaves us with a choice – will our story be better in present tense narration or in past tense? Here are some considerations and conventions that will help you decide.

1. Tense is independent of story setting

The first point to note is that the grammatical tense of the story has nothing to do with the time period in which the story is set. If your story is set in the future, it can be told in the grammatical past tense. And you can use present tense even if your story is set in the 17th Century.

2. Conventions

One consideration you can look at is the conventional wisdom on the subject. Past tense is seen as more traditional because, well, it *is* more traditional. But that doesn't mean it's old fashioned. It's just the way that stories have always been told.

Present tense is the new kid on the block. It's apparently more immediate and thrusts the reader more into the action. It gives the impression that the action is happening right now. Well, that's the theory anyway. Dissenters will say that this is nonsense and that there's nothing fuddy-duddy or less immediate about the past tense at all. The tense is just a grammatical form and doesn't imply that something happened long ago. It could have happened, like, one second ago, as opposed to right this very moment as our eyeballs are on the page.

We all grew up reading stories set in past tense and when we listened to stories told by parents or grandparents they were usually told in past tense. So past tense has become a signal to us that we are entering story mode.

My point of view is that past tense is so familiar to us as a storytelling mode that it becomes invisible as a tense. It allows us to immerse ourselves in the world of story. Present tense, on the other hand, can give an enhanced sense of immediacy and perhaps a faster pace (though, sometimes, somewhat breathless!).

3. Genre

Something else you can consider is what the current popular writers in your genre are using. For instance, in the Young Adult genre, there is a trend in favour of the present tense, perhaps because of the success of books like *The Hunger Games*, which are told in present tense.

Romance, crime and science fiction, on the other hand, tend to be solidly in past tense.

Literary fiction grants itself the freedom to use any tense, though present tense has become popular in recent years.

For most genres, it's unlikely a publisher will reject your story just because it's told in a tense that is not currently the rage. But do your own research here and check whether your favoured genre has any particular expectations of tense.

4. Instinct and feeling

The final way of deciding on a tense is just to go with gut instinct. Use the tense that your story wants to be told in. Yes, it's as inexact and mysterious as that. Your story will just feel better in a certain tense and point of view. The main thing is to start with what sounds right and then give yourself the freedom to change it later if you find that another tense and point of view seems more appropriate.

The grammar of tense

The first point to remember is that the tense of a sentence is indicated by the form of the verbs, for example, 'run' vs 'ran'. And the second point is that characters always speak from their present moment. This means that the verbs that give the tense of the sentence are the ones *outside* the quotation marks. You don't need to do anything to the verbs in the words spoken because these are always spoken from the character's present moment.

Take a look at the two versions of a short dialogue below. The first is in present tense and the second is in past tense. Notice how only the verbs outside the quotation marks change to indicate tense. The words actually spoken are unchanged.

Present tense

"What did you do for Christmas last year?" I ask.

She gives a glum expression and says, "Nothing much. Just sat around and exchanged polite insults."

The verbs 'did' and 'sat' in the words spoken are in past tense because the speakers are telling about something that happened in their past. However, the attribution verbs ('ask' and 'says') and the dialogue beat verb ('gives') are in the present, and these determine the tense of the narration.

Past tense

"What did you do for Christmas last year?" I asked.

She gave a glum expression and said, "Nothing much. Just sat around and exchanged polite insults."

In this past-tense example, the verbs in the direct speech are exactly the same as those in the present-tense example because the characters are still talking about something that happened in their past. However, the attribution verbs ('asked' and 'said') and the dialogue beat verb ('gave') are now in past tense.

Tip: Don't feel you have to make the correct choice on tense before you start writing. It is not uncommon for authors to start one way and then change their minds and rework what they've already written into a different tense. Sometimes you only really get a sense of what tense should be used once you're a fair distance down the track. So don't let this decision cause you to hesitate or sit too long thinking about it. Just start writing and experiment with different tenses and see which one works best.

The context of this lesson

Knowing about tenses is important because you will need to decide on a tense for your story and make sure the whole narrative (or at least the section or scene) follows this tense.

While some tense mistakes can be corrected by an editor, a manuscript with too many mistakes will be a signal to agents, publishers and readers that you are not in control of your narrative and they might stop reading. The matter of tense is also important because some genres expect a certain tense. Make sure you are familiar with the expectations and conventions of your genre.

Summary

Key points from this chapter:
- You need to decide whether you will narrate your story from the grammatical past or present. Future tense is hardly ever used.
- Past tense is seen as more traditional and present tense as more immediate and modern. But this is not a rule, only a consideration.
- Some genres of popular fiction have unwritten conventions regarding things like tense and point of view, so it can be a good idea to follow the trend.

Exercise

The written exercise for this topic will be given in the next chapter on point of view. In the meantime, simply reflect on your recent writing and consider these questions:

- Are you instinctively favouring either past or present narration?
- If so, what stories or authors are influencing you?
- If you are undecided about writing in the past or present, which one feels more comfortable or more aligned with your writing voice (understanding that this may change from story to story)?

CHAPTER 8

Choosing a Point of View

Point of view is another big decision you'll need to take in the early stages of writing any story. Point of view is pretty much what it says it is – the viewpoint from which the story is told. Think of it as the camera position in a movie. Does it follow one person around and show everything through his or her eyes? Or does it pull back a bit and take more of a birds-eye view of the action? And is there a narrator who tells the story and makes observations, kind of like a voiceover, or is everything told simply through the actions, speech and thought of the characters? These questions are all matters of point of view.

The place to start with all of this is to consider the grammatical 'person' who will tell the story. There are three possibilities:

- First-person – 'I' or 'we'
- Second-person – 'you'
- Third-person – 'he', 'she', 'it', 'they'

This all boils down to deciding whether you're going to write:

I ran through the forest, the wolves at *my* heels.

Or

You ran through the forest, the wolves at *your* heels.

Or

She ran through the forest, the wolves at *her* heels.

I think most people will agree that the second-person 'you' option isn't that realistic for fiction, except for short passages, so let's discard it for now. That leaves us having to choose between first-person and third-person.

Before we dive into the differences between the points of view we need to clarify what is meant by the term 'narrator' and 'point-of-view character'.

Narrators

The narrator is the actual or implied character or entity who tells the story. The identity of the narrator is a function of the point of view in which the story is told.

In first-person, the narrator is an actual character in the story – the 'I' who speaks. It is usually the protagonist but may also be an observer of the main action (e.g., Nick Carraway in *The Great Gatsby*). The first-person narrator is also known as a *participant narrator* because he or she takes part in the events of the story. As they are actual characters, first-person narrators can be subjective or unreliable – in other words, they might tell us things that are not completely true or which they believe to be true but are not. The relative ignorance of the participant narrator adds spice to the telling and means the reader has to do some work in figuring out what's really going on.

In third-person, the narrator can be either a character in the story or an unspecified entity who observes and narrates the events. The position of the narrator depends on whether the story is told from a limited third-person or an omniscient third-person point of view. We'll get into the differences between the two shortly. For now, just hold the idea that a third-person narrator can be either an actual character in the story (i.e., a participant narrator) or an abstract *non-participant* narrator.

Point-of-view characters

A point-of-view character (or POV character) is a character who narrates sections of a story or whose experiences, thoughts and impressions we follow. In first-person, this will be the 'I' character. In third-person, it will be the character who is central to a scene or chapter. Your protagonists are likely to be point-of-view characters because we experience the story literally through their point of view (their opinions, thoughts vantage point on the action, etc). Point-of-view characters are also called focus characters or viewpoint characters.

In first-person narration, there is only one viewpoint character – the 'I' who narrates. In third-person, there can be any number of viewpoint characters. We'll touch on point-of-view characters again towards the end of this module, but for now just remember that they are the characters whose thoughts, feelings and inner observations are shown. They don't just perform a function, they give us a viewpoint into the story through their own point of view. We feel what they feel, think what they think.

First-person point of view

In first-person, the story is told by a participant narrator speaking as 'I' or 'we'. The viewpoint is from within the narrator's head, giving us access to everything they see, hear, think and experience. The thoughts and experiences of other characters are not accessible to the reader, unless related through the observations of the narrator.

First-person narration is the closest to how we actually experience the world. We know what we're thinking or feeling, but we can never be sure of what others are thinking and feeling. All we have is their words and actions, and our interpretations of what those mean.

Here are some examples of the opening lines of novels written in the first person:

> I clasp the flask between my hands even though the warmth from the tea has long since leached into the frozen air. — *Catching Fire*, Suzanne Collins

> Whether I shall turn out to be the hero of my own life, or whether that station will be held by anybody else, these pages must show. — *David Copperfield*, Charles Dickens

Advantages of first-person

Because the narrator refers to themselves as 'I' and everything is experienced through their eyes, the reader in a sense *becomes* the narrator. At least on a subconscious level, the I of the story is the I of the reader. This makes first-person possibly the most intimate of the points of view. Not only does the reader identify as the 'I' of the narrator, but they totally depend on this one character for all their information. This creates an emotional bond between the protagonist and the reader that is perhaps stronger than what is the case with third-person narration. Note that this is not a rule, it's merely a principle or generalisation.

The capacity for first-person narration to get into the head of a single character is what makes it a popular choice for literary novels where the psychology of a single character is exposed in great detail.

It's also become a very popular point of view for young adult novels – think *The Hunger Games* (Suzanne Collins) and *Looking for Alaska* (John Green). First-person is chosen in this market because of its intensity and ability to focus on every thought and feeling – which is exactly the teen experience of life. This is not to say you *have* to write in first-person for young adults, just that it's worth your consideration.

Limitations of first-person

The intimacy of first-person is also its great limitation. If you are telling a story through the eyes of a single character your reader can only know what the character knows. Events that take place out of sight of the narrator are strictly off-limits. So too are the thoughts and feelings of other people. You can show their reactions, as seen through the eyes of the narrator, but their inner lives are inaccessible.

This can be a challenge if there's something you want the reader to know that the narrator doesn't know. For instance, you can't let the reader know that an army is advancing on the castle under cover of night as the hero lies peacefully asleep. The first that the hero, and the reader, will find out about it is when all hell breaks loose at sunrise. Now this might not actually be a limitation because the reader perhaps doesn't need to know the army is marching until the arrows start to fly. In this case, the limitation of first-person lends itself to the creation of added tension and big surprises. You just need to be aware, as the writer, that if you choose first-person you are going to have to be disciplined about what information you share with the reader. If you want to write a sweeping epic told from many perspectives, then first-person is probably not the best choice.

Note that you can get around this limitation by using more than one 'I' narrator in a novel, but this is rare and takes some skill. Each narrator would have to have his or her own chapters so as not to confuse the reader about who they are following. John Green's *Will Grayson, Will Grayson* and Paula Hawkins' *The Girl on the Train* are good examples of this approach.

To summarise, the advantages of first-person narration:
• Easy to create emotional involvement by the reader.
And the disadvantages of first-person:
• Limited to what can be observed or thought by the narrator.
• The reader has to work a bit harder to interpret motivations, plot, etc. (though this could be an advantage if you want to raise suspense by limiting what the audience knows).

Third-person point of view

Third-person uses the pronouns 'he', 'she', 'they', 'their', etc. There are two main types of third-person narration – unlimited (omniscient) and limited.

Third-person omniscient

The third-person omniscient narrator is not a participant in the story but is an abstract observer. This is probably the narrative voice you're instinctively most familiar with as it is perhaps the most widely used point of view in classic literature.

There's a reason why it has been so popular – it gives the author god-like powers to know and see everything that is happening with the story. The narrator has the freedom to see into every character's thoughts and knows what's going to happen in the future. An omniscient narrator can shift focus to many different characters, describing their thoughts and actions. The narrator can pass judgement on characters as well as on the politics and morality of the society in which the story is set.

In omniscient narration, the reader has a sense of assurance that everything that happens in the work is under the author's control. This makes omniscient narration the most objective and trustworthy viewpoint and affords the author the oppor-tunity to tell the reader everything they need to know to understand a situation. Contrast this with authors of literary fiction who choose first-person narration precisely to avoid sustaining the illusion that the world is stable and knowable.

Jane Austen's *Pride and Prejudice* is written in omniscient narration. Here is the start of the first scene, containing what is surely one of the most famous opening lines in literature.

It is a truth, universally acknowledged, that a single man in possession of a good fortune, must be in want of a wife. However little known the feelings or views of such a man may be on his first entering a neighbourhood, this truth is so well fixed in the minds of the surrounding families, that he is considered as the rightful property of some or other of their daughters.

"My dear Mr. Bennett," said his lady to him one day, "have you heard that Netherfield Park is let at last?"

Mr. Bennett replied that he had not.

"But it is," returned she; "for Mrs. Long has just been there, and she told me all about it."

Mr. Bennett made no answer.

Take a look at those first two sentences again. Who is it who states that delightful truth about wealthy men and marriage? It is not Mr or Mrs Bennett but rather a non-participant, abstract narrator who speaks from the vantage point of the author. This narrator has the freedom to pass comment on the thoughts and behaviours of the characters and can bring in information from anywhere plausible. For instance, if they wanted to state what Napoleon Bonaparte was doing at the same time as Mrs Bennett was sipping her tea, they would be able to do that quite comfortably.

If Austen had lived in more recent times she might have opted for first-person narration. However, she would not have been able to make that opening statement unless she made it part of the thinking process of the protagonist, Elizabeth. Here are some of the changes she would have had to make, giving myself some licence to embellish where necessary (additions in italics):

It is a truth, universally acknowledged, that a single man in possession of a good fortune, must be in want of a wife. *That's what Mother believes though she has not said it in as many words. I pity this man of good fortune!* However little known his feelings or views may be on his first entering a neighbourhood, this truth is so well fixed in the minds of the surrounding families, that he is considered as the rightful property of some or other of their daughters.

"My dear Mr. Bennett," said *Mother* to him one day, "have you heard that Netherfield Park is let at last?"

Father replied that he had not.

"But it is," returned she; "for Mrs. Long has just been there, and she told me all about it."

Father made no answer.

Notice how I had to add material to put the opening comment in Elizabeth's words. And see how this changes the focus and swings everything to centre on the 'I' character, Elizabeth. Now she has to be in every scene, whereas in the original text, she doesn't appear until Chapter 2. This is what I was referring to earlier about the emotional intensity of first-person narration. It's all about one character, whereas with third-person omniscient you can have several characters and an abstract narrator.

Advantages of omniscient point of view:
• No restriction on the information you can give.
• Can portray the inner and outer lives of many characters.
• Creates a sense of order and trust – the narrator can be trusted to tell the truth (unlike first-person where the narrator may be unreliable).
• Readers don't have to work too hard to figure out plot or character motives.

Disadvantages of omniscient point of view:

- Readers might be less emotionally involved because everything is mediated through the narrator who is one step removed from the action, and readers don't have to invest any effort in interpreting characters' moral qualities.

Third-person limited point of view

Third-person limited is written in the grammatical third person (he, she, it), but only shows the viewpoint of one character, so it's essentially first-person expressed as third-person. The author reveals all the characteristics and motivations of one character and stays out of the heads of all the others. The only way the author can let the reader know what other characters are thinking or feeling is to convey a sense of this in dialogue or in the actions and expressions of the other characters.

The narrator in third-person limited is not the abstract narrator of omniscient narration but is an actual character – a participant narrator. The narrator is the same as in first-person narration, so the 'I' of a first-person narration would become the 'he' or 'she' of third-person limited. However, because third-person has a slight distancing effect, it's like we're watching the scene from over the character's shoulder rather than looking directly through their eyes. The golden rule with third-person limited is that you can only show what the viewpoint character knows, perceives, remembers and experiences. You can't tell the reader anything directly, as you can with an omniscient narrator.

So why would an author choose limited point of view if it has so many limitations? Why not just stick with 'I' and have the advantage of the greater immediacy of first-person, or go large with omniscient point of view?

The answer is that limited POV combines some of the advantages of first-person and omniscient in creative ways:

- It focuses attention on one character (as in first-person) and can create more of an emotional bond than is common with omniscient.
- It enables you to have more than one point-of-view character (as in omniscient) while keeping much of the intimacy and immediacy of first-person.

Let's look at these points in a bit more detail.

1. Focusing attention on one character

Third-person limited enables you to write in third-person for audiences who prefer this point of view, while maintaining most of the advantages of first-person. You get more or less the same intimacy and emotional bonding as you would with first-person because you stay with the thoughts and perceptions of the focus character. The reader's attention is not split by following several different characters' perceptions in the same scene or chapter.

An often-cited example of third-person limited narration is the Harry Potter series. It is written in grammatical third-person, past tense, and it only shows what Harry is able to see or know. This creates the emotional bonding with Harry that makes him such a memorable character. Here's a sample from Book 2:

> Harry went back to his toast. Of course, he thought bitterly, Uncle Vernon was talking about the stupid dinner

party. He'd been talking of nothing else for a fortnight.
— *Harry Potter and the Chamber of Secrets*, JK Rowling

From this extract you can't tell whether the narration is omniscient or limited third-person – it's only when you read a few pages that you realise you only ever know Harry's thoughts and you don't know anything he doesn't know. This means it's third-person limited.

2. More than one point-of-view character

This is the real superpower of limited point of view. If you like the close-up, intimate effect of first-person but you want to have more than one first-person character, you're going to have problems if you tell the story in grammatical first-person. The only way around it is to have, say, a maximum of two 'I' characters and then separate them into alternating chapters. But this is not an easy thing to do.

The alternative is to switch to third-person but keep the focus limited to *one point-of-view character at a time*. Then all you do is separate each focus character into separate scenes or chapters, clearly indicating who it is we're following. For instance, say you have two brothers – Jack and Pete – and you want to show how each one experiences an event differently. You could have one scene where you begin by naming the character, saying something like, 'Jack wandered through the woods, cold and hungry.' Then you refer to him as 'he' for the rest of the scene. And then in the next scene you signal a change of focal character by saying something like, 'Pete loaded the rifle and aimed at the dim figure approaching through the woods'. After that you refer to Pete as 'he' or 'him'. So the same pronouns refer to two different people in two separate scenes. And you can do this with more than just two characters.

This is similar to the tactic George RR Martin used to cram so many point-of-view characters into *Game of Thrones*. Take Book 1 (*A Song of Fire and Ice*) for example. Each chapter is titled with the name of the character who is the focal character of that chapter. In this way, the story is told from the viewpoints of eight protagonists (Ned, Catelyn, Sansa, Arya, Bran, Jon Snow, Tyrion, and Daenerys) without causing confusion.

That's a lot of focus characters, but it works because the reader is clear about who they are meant to focus on and bond with in each chapter. Note that, technically, *Game of Thrones* is narrated in limited *omniscient* rather than limited third-person, but you don't need to worry about that distinction just yet. The main point to get is that limiting your third-person or omniscient narration to follow just one character at a time gives you the freedom to include many focal characters.

Advanced point of view: Limited omniscient

Wish you could have the advantages of limited third-person *and* have an abstract narrator to make omniscient observations? Well, turns out there's a point of view for that – limited omniscient, also called combination or combo point of view.

In combo point of view, you adopt the abstract narrator of full omniscient for when you want to give the audience necessary information or describe things happening off-stage somewhere, but then you zoom in close and follow only one point-of-view character per scene or chapter. It's like a movie shot that begins wide-angle but then zooms in and stays with one character throughout the scene.

The *Game of Thrones* books offer excellent examples of combo point of view. Each chapter is told from the point of view of a different character. On the surface, it looks very much like third-person limited except for the fact that occasional comments and observations clearly come from an abstract narrator rather than the point-of-view character. It's not always easy to pick up on the difference between limited omniscience and limited third-person, so if this feels headache-inducing, leave it for now and only refer back to it if you ever find yourself wondering how to fit multiple point-of-view characters into a novel.

Distinguishing between omniscient and third-person limited

Telling the difference between omniscient third-person and limited third-person is not always easy because the lines can get a bit blurred. The main thing to ask is: Does the narrator have more information than the point-of-view character? If so, it's omniscient.

The difference can be shown in these short examples:

Limited: A round, black stone caught her eye and she picked it up.

Omniscient: A round, black stone caught her eye and she picked it up, *little knowing it was the sorcerer's stone that would summon darkness back into the world.*

Limited: As Joe sat reading his book, he felt a draught on the back of his neck and a chill ran down his spine.

Omniscient: As Joe sat reading his book, the door softly opened and *the wraith seeped into the room and came to hover just behind his back.* A chill ran down his spine.

In the examples above, the statements in italics convey information that the characters do not know, so it's the omniscient author-narrator who is giving this information.

Point of view and genres

When choosing a point of view for your story, one thing that you should consider is whether the genre you are writing in has an expected or trending point of view and tense. While I believe an author should write in the viewpoint and tense that suits the story best, I also believe it's a good idea to see if one can meet the expectations of one's audience, at least if one wants to sell a good many books.

So here are some pointers on genres and point of view. Please be aware that these expectations can change at any time, so always do your homework first and see what the top authors in your genre are using.

Young adult and new adult

First-person is popular in these markets because of the emotional intensity that this point of view brings. Especially since *The Hunger Games*, first-person present is the fashion. However, these are only trends and are not absolute rules. For instance, *Harry Potter* is third-person past tense.

Mystery and detective

First-person is a possible choice because the limited perspective enables you to keep information from the reader for longer. Third-person combo is also a good choice, enabling you to show the crime-fighters in omniscient and the criminal in third-person limited. Or you could use ordinary limited viewpoint throughout.

Science fiction

The general expectation is for omniscient, past tense. First-person is not generally used unless the author is aiming for a more literary effect.

Romance

Third-person limited, past tense, with two point-of-view characters – the heroine and hero.

Thrillers and other popular fiction

Any third-person point of view, past tense. Psychological thrillers, on the other hand, tend to favour first-person because it allows the portrayal of intense emotions and thoughts.

Literary

Any point of view. Present tense is fashionable (but not necessary).

Once again, these are not unbreakable rules, just general trends at the time of writing this course. The advice, as always, is to do your research and to see what the leading lights in your favourite genre are doing. Be aware that mainstream publishers in some genres do have fairly inflexible rules about what point of view and tense they will publish in. For instance, if you're thinking of writing a bodice-ripper romance, you'll almost certainly have to write it in third-person, past tense, from the perspective of the heroine and the hero.

Troubleshooter: Head-hopping

Earlier in this chapter I introduced the concept of point-of-view or viewpoint characters. These are the characters whose thoughts, feelings and observations are shown, as opposed to those characters who just perform a function and who have no viewpoint on the story.

Questions around viewpoint characters don't usually arise in first-person narration because there is usually only one viewpoint character throughout the story. In third-person, however, you can have many viewpoint characters – and that's where the complications come on. Take a look at this example:

> *Jim and the briefcase*
>
> Jim gripped the leather briefcase on his lap and prayed that it contained exactly the right amount. One finger for every dollar short, they'd promised. On the other side of the table, Madame Zungu gloated over Jim's discomfort. She wondered whether she should have Ivan cut off a finger before they even started counting – just to send a message. Oh, that would be so satisfying. Ivan stood solidly with his blue eyes fixed coldly on Jim. Such a timid little man deserved a taste of the blade, he thought. He took the switchblade out of his pocket and flicked it open, just to make him squirm.

Whose point of view are we in? Everybody's and nobody's. This kind of uncontrolled narrative where the point of view skips randomly from one character's inner experience to another is called head-hopping. In this scene, the story is told from Jim's perspective, then Madame Zungu's, and then Ivan's.

In limited third-person, head-hopping commonly arises when authors jump from one viewpoint character to another within the same scene or even within the same paragraph. The result is that the reader doesn't know who they are meant to follow and get confused about who is experiencing the situation. So if you're writing in limited third-person with multiple point-of-view characters, make sure you tell each scene from the perspective of just one character. In the 'Jim and the briefcase' example, we could fix the head-hopping by rewriting the scene from Jim's perspective alone, leaving him to deduce the thoughts and intentions of the others by their actions and expressions.

In omniscient point of view, head-hopping commonly occurs when the author drops out of the abstract voice of the god-like narrator and starts narrating in the voice of different characters. While the abstract narrator is free to describe the thoughts and feelings of any character, they are not free to convey these thoughts and feelings *in the words and voices* of the characters. When this happens, they are slipping out of the single, abstract voice of the omniscient narrator into the multiple voices of third-person limited. They are moving from being an abstract narrator to a participant narrator. This can be a bit tricky to spot. Here's a scene written in omniscient point of view without head-hopping:

Andy gripped the wheel and glanced at Shirley. He felt sure he was on the right road. Mostly sure. But if she made one more comment about looking at a map he'd stop and tell her to walk. He was mostly sure of that too.

> Shirley stared straight ahead of her down the dusty farm road. Her rage was giving way to a cold sobriety. If he was too damn proud to look at a map and he ended up getting them lost somewhere she knew she'd leave. Perhaps she had already left and that was the coldness that was coming in. There was no stopping it now.

Although both Andy's and Shirley's feelings and thoughts are shown, they are narrated in the abstract voice of the narrator. The narrator is telling the story, not any of the characters. Now take a look at this version, where narration slips into the viewpoint of each character:

> Andy gripped the wheel and glanced at Shirley. I'm on the right road, he thought. I'm sure of it. But if she makes one more comment about looking at a map I'll stop and tell her to walk. He was mostly sure of that too.
>
> Shirley stared straight ahead of her down the dusty farm road. She felt her rage give way to a cold sobriety. If he's too damn proud to look at a map and he ends up getting us lost somewhere, I'll leave him. Simple as that. Perhaps it's already happened, she thought, as that familiar, numbing coldness came seeping in. There was no stopping it now.

Notice how the narrator descends from the abstract, non-participant position and enters the perspectives of the two characters. The reader is asked to identify with both characters as narrators, which becomes confusing. Even more confusing is the fact that there are still elements of the abstract narrator's omniscient comments in the text, so we have both non-participant and participant narrators in the same scene.

Head-hopping can be a tricky concept to grasp so don't feel you have to master it right now. Just keep the following simple principles in mind:

- Give point of view only to your principal characters and not to every character that appears.
- In third-person limited, stick to one viewpoint character for each scene or chapter. Don't jump from one viewpoint character's perspective to another within a scene or paragraph.
- In omniscient point of view, relate the thoughts and feelings of any character, but do this in the voice of the abstract narrator. Don't drop into the words, pacing, and voice of any particular character.

The context of this lesson

Knowing your options regarding point of view empowers you to choose the best point of view for your story. It's one of the key decisions you'll need to make as you take a story from rough draft to publishable manuscript. Some genres insist on a particular point of view, so agents and publishers in these genres might not even look at your manuscript if it doesn't follow the convention.

Another good reason to begin mastering point of view is that many of the technical problems you will face when writing a longer work will have something to do with point of view. You need to understand the limitations of your chosen point of view and the tactics for working with these limitations and turning them to your advantage.

Summary

Point of view refers to who is telling or narrating a story:

- First-person: Uses the pronoun 'I'. The narrator is a participant narrator (an actual character in the story). First-person creates intimacy and character intensity but can't show anything the 'I' character doesn't directly experience or know.
- Third-person omniscient: Uses pronouns he/she/it. The narrator is abstract and non-participant (not an actual character). The omniscient narrator is god-like and can give information about anyone and anything.
- Third-person limited: Uses pronouns he/she/it. The narrator is a participant narrator. The limitation is that you can only show what the viewpoint character knows or experiences.
- Limited-omniscient/combo: Uses pronouns he/she/it. Combines omniscient third-person for brief passages of abstract narration with limited third-person to follow particular characters.
- In third-person, give point of view only to your main characters (i.e. stay out of the heads of minor characters). And avoid head hopping.

Exercises

1. Write a scene

Write a scene or part of a scene at least half a page long. Write in the point of view and tense of your choice.

Subject: Try to write a scene that builds on the story you are already working on for this course. For example, take the character from your story premise and then put them in a situation where they meet someone, go somewhere, have a conversation or face some kind of a challenge. Freewrite on what happens.

Story prompts: If you haven't decided on what to write or just want to try something completely new, use these scene prompts for ideas:

- Someone hands over a briefcase (or bag or box) containing something of high value, e.g., ransom money, drug money, state secrets, plutonium, a kidney.
- Someone hires a private investigator to investigate a sensitive matter.
- Children find something strange in the woods.
- A husband or wife tells their spouse the marriage is over.
- A chance encounter that will lead to a romance or to something sinister.
- Someone with a dark past or present (e.g., gangster, murderer, corrupt politician, mafia boss, war criminal) performs a random act of kindness.
- An alienated child or teenager experiences a moment of connection or unexpected affirmation.

2. Transpose a scene

Now take the same scene and transpose it to a new point of view and a new tense. For example, if you've written in third-person present, rework it to first-person past.

3. Reflection

Reflect on the result of the exercise and comment on how the second version differs from the first in terms of mood, pacing, texture, limitations and any other factors that stand out. Did changing the tense and point of view improve the piece or do you feel the original worked better?

CHAPTER 9

Showing vs Telling

If there's one piece of writing advice you'll get about a zillion times in your writing career, it's this: *Show don't tell.*

But what does it mean?

Well, let's begin with Telling. Telling is when you give your readers direct information about a character or part of the story. For instance, you'll say, 'Joe was very tall'. You're telling them a fact about his size and the reader doesn't need to use their imagination to figure anything out.

Showing, on the other hand, is when you use sensory details and actions to convey meaning rather than stating things directly. So instead of saying 'Joe was very tall' you could say, 'Joe stooped as he walked through the door'. You're asking the reader to figure out that Joe is tall rather than telling them directly.

The magic of showing is that it engages the reader's imagination in a way that telling does not. And when readers have to imagine things for themselves, they develop an emotional bond with the characters and the story as a whole. Showing makes stories come alive. It's the thing that separates creative writing from other forms of writing. So can you guess which of the four modes of writing are involved in the question of showing vs telling?

If you said that showing is narrative and telling is exposition, you'd be correct. Narrative is communicating a story in a way that heightens emotional involvement and transports the reader into a world of the imagination. Exposition is just giving facts and saying what happened.

As fiction and creative non-fiction are predominantly narrative writing modes, you need to pay attention to the balance of showing vs telling and make sure you're not overdoing the telling. If all you're doing is telling, then you're not writing a story, you're writing an essay.

Here's a short passage written as telling and as showing. Notice which one engages you more.

> Telling: I heard footsteps in the dark behind me and began to feel terrified.
>
> Showing: I stopped abruptly and heard a single footfall behind me. It was him; I knew it! My heart hammered in my chest and I stifled a scream.

Which version draws you in and seems more immediate? I'm betting it's the second one. Now let's take a longer passage and examine it a bit more closely.

> I'll never get this right, Jinn thought. He knew he had to find the right words to the spell or the demon would find the sacred amulet and become invincible. He kept repeating lines he'd memorised, growing more and more frustrated as each one failed and the howling of

the demon grew louder. He felt stupid and regretted ever trying to become a mage and doing battle with the Dark.

On the surface, this looks like an OK bit of fiction, but is it living up to its potential? Notice how the writer tells us exactly what Jinn is feeling and thinking. This positions us as observers, watching from a distance. We never really get inside the character's experience as everything is told as a collection of facts, for instance:

- The demon would become 'invincible'.
- Jinn became 'more and more frustrated'.
- He 'felt stupid'.
- He 'regretted' trying to become a mage.

All this is telling us what is happening and what the character is thinking and feeling. It's just bland, abstract exposition. It looks like fiction, but it's rather a poor specimen.

So let's try a rewrite and see if we can replace some of that boring exposition with narration.

I'll never get this right! Jinn closed his eyes and feverishly scanned his memory for the words of the demon-banishing spell. Pages and pages of the old grimoire flickered across his vision as the howling outside the church rose to a fever pitch. *"Exite malum spiritus!"* he shouted. Nothing. *"Abeo demonas!"* And still the howling grew. Jinn pressed his hands over his ears and sank to the floor with a whimper. Foolish boy! To think he could ever be a mage and stop the Dark.

In this passage, Jinn's experiences are shown directly so we can experience them for ourselves. For instance, in the first sentence we have an actual thought – 'I'll never get this right!' – and from this we deduce his fear and frustration. We aren't *told* he is frustrated, we *feel* it.

Instead of being told that Jinn had to find the right words to the spell or bad things would happen, we are shown his feverish search through pages and pages of the old grimoire as howling rages outside. The sensory details convey the urgency and danger – we don't need to be told it. And instead of being told that Jinn repeated lines of spells we now get the actual lines in direct speech. That's much more powerful.

When we are told something we are outside of the experience, but when we see the character's reactions and hear his or her thoughts directly we *create the experience for ourselves* and thus become part of the adventure rather than bystanders.

Here are some more examples of showing vs telling:

Telling: He felt stupid.

Showing: Oh, what a fool! he thought.

In the example above, the 'showing' passage tells the reader what he thought, but it's not telling the reader what the character feels. The reader must come to this realisation themselves.

Telling: As she walked down the road it began to rain.

Showing: As she walked an icy drizzle began to sift down from the flat, grey sky, turning the bare trees along the road black and stark in the gathering gloom.

In this example, the 'showing' passage does include some telling – it tells us an icy drizzle is sifting down, but the choice of words is also creating a mood or emotional tone. In other words, it's *showing* us an emotion while *telling* us about the weather.

I think the showing versions are certainly more evocative, but does this mean you should never tell and always show? Brilliant question! Let's investigate.

When to tell rather than show

If you compare the examples of telling and showing I've given, you'll notice that the showing passages are longer and more detailed than the telling. The telling versions read quickly, while the showing versions take longer and slow things down, drawing the reader in.

The simple fact is that sometimes you don't want to slow the story down and you just want to give the reader some information. For instance:

- To move quickly between scenes
- To summarise events
- To move your characters from one place to another
- To give backstory or historical context
- To describe a minor character

It's also quite OK to tell the reader what a character is feeling if you don't particularly need the reader to slow down and feel it for themselves. For example:

She hurried down the road and arrived at the bank, relieved and breathless, a minute before closing time.

Instead of making a rule that says you should always show and not tell, rather focus on mastering both forms of expression so you can use them deliberately. Often, it's perfectly OK to be direct and say, 'He loved her with all his heart'. But sometimes it's more effective to be indirect and show the evidence of his love and let the audience come to their own conclusions: 'He stammered and blushed when she said hello'.

To write a story completely in showing mode is unrealistic and undesirable. It's too laborious, both for the writer and the reader. So it's quite natural to have passages of exposition where you supply necessary information or whisk the reader off to a new scene. Telling only really becomes a problem when it's obvious that the writer is taking shortcuts and not going to the trouble of engaging the reader's imagination.

How to 'show don't tell'

Here are some pointers for writing lively, engaging narrative that shows rather than tells:

1. Reduce filter words

Filter words are verbs that separate the reader from the action. They filter the action through the perspective of a narrator, reminding us that what we're reading is being told by someone rather than being experienced directly.

Filter words include words like 'heard', 'felt', 'smelled', 'wondered', 'thought', and 'saw'. They are all basic sensory words. They seem necessary, but often they're not. Here are some examples of passages with and without filtering. The filter words are in italics.

> With filtering: I walked in the garden and *smelled* the scent of rose and honeysuckle.

> Without filtering: The scent of rose and honeysuckle filled the air as I walked in the garden.

*

With filtering: Kayla_realised_she had to tell Baron and *felt* dreadful about it. She *knew* it would hurt him terribly. But she'd *become aware* months before that she was no longer in love with him. She *wondered* guiltily if she was incapable of loving one person forever.

Without filtering: Kayla dreaded telling Baron. The news would be like a knife in the heart. But she couldn't avoid it – she'd fallen out of love with him months before. Perhaps she was incapable of loving one person forever.

Do you see how unnecessary all those filter words really are? They keep us at a distance and stop us from really feeling the sensory detail.

2. Use concrete rather than abstract language

Telling is a kind of summarised description – it cuts down on the number of words used, but in so doing it loses a lot of detail. We can say that telling tends to use abstract words and phrases while showing is more concrete and detailed.

Take a look at this example again:

Telling: As she walked down the road it began to rain.

Showing: As she walked an icy drizzle began to sift down from the flat grey sky, turning the bare trees along the road black and stark in the gathering gloom.

The word 'rain' is quite general and non-specific – what, exactly, is the feeling of rain? And what kind of rain is it? Think about it – you never actually experience rain. What you experience is the result of rain – wet, dripping, icy pinpricks, stinging droplets, warm splashes, drumming, trickling. 'Rain' is abstract, but 'great plashes of blood-warm water' is more concrete and embodied. You can feel it.

If you're using words like these, you know you're being abstract: 'Injustice', 'isolation', 'anger', 'suffering', 'peace', 'exploitation', 'fear', 'love'. If you've ever been in love, you'll know it's the most real and wonderful thing ever. But you never actually feel love. You feel a beating heart, a warm glow, an upwelling of laughter, the delight of a smile, and words blurted out without thinking. 'Love' is abstract and general. It points to a category of experience, but it's not a lived experience.

Abstract: She loved him.

Concrete: She blushed at the mere thought of him.

Once again, it's not that abstract language is bad, it's just that you want to make sure you're not overusing it and distancing the reader from the experience. The important thing is to get a balance between showing and telling, with a bias towards showing. More narrative, less exposition.

3. Reduce emotion-explaining words

Emotion-explaining words are nouns or adjectives describing states of being. For example, 'happy', 'sad', 'angry', 'excited', 'frustrated', 'love', 'joy', 'disgust', 'bliss'.

You might notice that these are also abstract words. They describe categories of feeling rather than specific felt experiences. When you find yourself using emotion-explaining words, pause to see if actions, gestures and speech might be more effective.

Telling: Little Jess was *so excited* when the Christmas tree lights were turned on.

Showing: Little Jess gasped and clapped her hands when the Christmas tree lights were turned on.

4. Use body language, gestures, and actions

People don't only communicate in words – they use body language, gestures and actions. So instead of telling us someone is angry, show them going red in the face or the muscles in their necks bulging. If they're sad, let their shoulders slump and let them say sad things. Or just let them speak slowly with downcast eyes. Or say nothing at all.

If they're excited, let them do a little dance or speak too fast.

If they're cruel, let them sit and pull the wings off flies.

5. Use dialogue

Instead of telling the reader what someone is doing, thinking, or feeling, see if you can put it into dialogue. Or have another character comment on your focus character.

Telling: Mandy behaved like a real little brat.

Showing: "You little horror!" exclaimed Mother, glaring at Mandy.

Showing: "That Mandy is a bit of a brat, don't you think?" said Miss Jolly to Mr Jimson.

6. Clean up info dumps

An info dump is a big old heap of exposition that doesn't belong where it's put. It's just plain boring to read and gets in the way of the real action. Readers want a story, not an essay.

Info dumps are common problems with novice writers who feel they have to give the reader all the backstory and character details up front. The drama of the moment gets lost in unnecessary detail and explanation. In technical terms, the narrative is being diluted by the exposition. To clear up an info dump, ask yourself these questions:

- Does the reader need all this information?
- Can part of it be moved elsewhere? (i.e., can the exposition be separated from the narrative?)
- Can this information be dramatised or conveyed in dialogue or action in a way that lets readers figure out the meaning for themselves?

The exposition reduction process

You can use the six points I've outlined to fix any passage of writing that has too much exposition. Here's how it works as a process:

Step 1: Begin by underlining all the filter words, emotion-explaining words and abstract language.

Step 2: Note places where body language, actions and dialogue could help convey meaning (add action prompts in square brackets).

Step 3: Then circle or highlight any info dumps that need to be broken up.

Let's try this on an example.

Miss Jones, the teacher, was a real tyrant. She made her students' lives a misery by doing everything she could to make them feel stupid and by regularly beating them with a ruler. She had been at the school for 30 years and had never married.

To run the exposition reduction process, I'll begin by underlining all the telling words and expressions.

Then I'll use square brackets to insert notes of where I could possibly convey information through action or gesture. Here, I reckon we can show her being a tyrant with some action, and we can also perhaps use action to show how she makes the children feel stupid. We can also rework the fact that she likes to beat the children as some kind of action.

Step 3 is to circle or mark any info dumps. As I see it, that last sentence gives unnecessary backstory that detracts from the potential drama of the piece. So I'm going to put it in italics to mark it as an info dump. You might well have ideas for how it can be part of the drama of the scene, but for the purposes of this example I'm just going to mark it for deletion. If I really need to give this information, I'll find a better way of saying it later.

This is how the piece looks once I've marked it up:

Miss Jones, the <u>teacher</u>, was a real <u>tyrant</u> [action]. She made her students' lives a <u>misery</u> by doing <u>everything she could</u> to make them <u>feel stupid</u> [action/dialogue] and by <u>regularly beating</u> them [action] with a ruler. *She had been at the school for 30 years and had never married.*

Now here's my attempt at reworking the passage:

From the other classes came the sounds of boisterous play but in Class 9b the children sat in nervous silence. The clock on the wall at the front of the class showed 8:29. At precisely 8:30 the door swung open and Miss Jones marched in. She dropped her Samsonite briefcase on the table with a loud thud and then picked up the blackboard ruler. "Homework out," she ordered, and smacked the end of the ruler against the palm of her left hand.

I think that works better. You get a sense that Miss Jones is a tyrant without it being overtly stated. The fear of the children is evident from their silent waiting. There are now some actions (the children waiting, Miss Jones dropping the briefcase with a thud and smacking the ruler on her palm). And there's a short piece of direct speech that makes her more real and alive. The information about her not being married and having been a teacher for 30 years was not essential to this scene, so I've left it out.

Showing vs telling example

Here's another example of a passage being reworked to bring in more showing. Read the original version below and then consider the questions that follow it.

Getting into his car, detective Max Miller reviews the message again. It informs him that there has been a murder in the south of London at the corner of Gillingham and Victoria Street. He puts his siren on top of the vehicle and speeds away. This situation is not new to him. On the contrary, this is his 21st year working for the

Police Homicide unit. His work consumes all his time and this in turn affects his personal life. Well, the little of it he still has. He nearly never talks to his oldest son, Joseph, anymore. John also has a daughter, Emily, who is presently 16 years old. His wife, Paula, is a High school counsellor. Their relationship has been distant for quite some time now.

You might have already picked up on some issues in this passage that make it less effective than it could be. Keep those in mind and then consider these questions:

- Is the drama of the piece being watered down by filter words, emotion-explaining words and abstract words and phrases?
- Are there any places where body language and gestures could convey emotions better than words?
- Are there any info dumps?
- Are there pieces of exposition that just sound dull and which call for more of a narrative (showing) approach?

In my opinion, most of the piece is really an info dump. The core drama – Detective Max Miller being called to a murder scene and racing off in his car – is diluted by unnecessary exposition and backstory. The solution is to see how much of that telling can be converted into showing, and to consider how much of the backstory can simply be moved out of the scene.

I've attempted a rewrite below. Note that I wrote it to fix the language issues and didn't really address the question of whether all that background family information was necessary. I kept it in to see how it would read if presented in more of a narrative style. You can decide for yourself if it works or if it should be moved out of the scene.

Detective Max Miller jumps into his car and checks the message again. Homicide – corner of Gillingham and Victoria. He smacks the siren onto the roof of his car and speeds away. The thrill of a new case – there's nothing quite like it, not even now, after 21 years with the Homicide Unit. All his concerns, his attachments, for a while, forgotten. His family has got used to not having him around. Joseph is almost finished college, studying some kind of commerce degree that will probably make him wealthy one day or bored as hell. And Emily, just a short while ago she was a young girl who would run to the door to welcome her father home from work. Now she barely raises an eye when he walks through the door. His wife, Paula, has been wondering whether she should have an affair.

Does that read better? If so, why?

What can you deduce about the detective's family life that isn't stated explicitly in the text?

Do you have any thoughts about making this scene even more effective?

Note that there are still some passages of straight exposition, for example telling the reader that Miller's wife is thinking of having an affair, but this also serves the purpose of showing that his family life is falling apart. So don't feel you have to get rid of all telling. Just aim for a balance. Sometimes, telling tells at one level but shows at another.

The context of this lesson

The art of showing rather than telling is perhaps the most essential skill you will need to learn as a writer of fiction. Showing breathes life into your story. It evokes imagination and interpretation, drawing readers in and getting them emotionally involved. Agents, publishers and readers can immediately see whether you are mastering this discipline or whether you are just relying on 'telling' to give information. A few skilful passages of showing in your opening pages can win you a publishing deal. In fact, publishers are willing to overlook other faults if your showing is brilliant.

Summary

Key points from this chapter:
- Telling is when the author tells the reader what a character is feeling or gives the reader direct information. Showing is when the author allows the reader to deduce emotions, motives and other information from the behaviour or speech of the characters.
- Telling is exposition – explaining or giving information. Showing is narration – telling a story.
- Showing is good for dramatising a scene and drawing the reader in. Telling is useful when you want to give the reader information without slowing the pace by dramatising it (for example, to move quickly between scenes, to summarise or telescope events, to give background information or to get your character from one place to another).

- To show rather than tell: Cut filter words, reduce emotion-explaining words, use concrete rather than abstract language, include body language and actions, add dialogue, and clean up info dumps.

Exercises

1. Rewrite a scene

The *PI Blues* piece below is suffering terribly from an overdose of telling. Rewrite it so that it comes alive. You can change aspects of it to suit your imagination, but do include the essential story idea – a divorced private investigator, with no work and low self-esteem, receives a call. Other than that, go wild. You can even change the gender of the characters. Use all your skills of narration to make this an irresistible read.

PI Blues

My name is Jonas Blewett, a private eye. I used to live in Malibu until my wife divorced me, and now I've been renting a dingy room in downtown LA. My wife was my partner in crime, so to speak, and when she gave me the boot things just fell apart. When I left I took the nameplate off the door of our agency and brought it with me. Now it hangs on the shabby wooden door to my office. *Blewett & Blewett, Private Investigators*, it reads.

The office is a small room with a desk, phone and three chairs. When it is quiet the phone can go for days or even weeks without ringing. Then I start thinking the phone isn't working and I end up calling the phone company and asking them to test the line. But disappointingly, it's always working perfectly.

Today is one of those days. I pick up the phone and listen for the dial tone. No problem there, unfortunately. I decide to go down to the coffee shop on the corner. Truth is, it's only partly for the coffee. It's also damn lonely sitting here all day. At the coffee shop I order a double espresso and a croissant. I can't really afford it but what the hell. As I'm sitting there I start to wonder if the phone is ringing in the office. Just my luck if it does. A pretty woman sits at the window counter a short way from me. I start to think of ways to say hi, but then I'm reminded of my greying hair and somewhat haggard face and the fact that I haven't looked after myself since the divorce. Never had a reason to really, though it would be nice to meet someone. And nice to get a case. I wonder if that phone is ringing. Should I drink my coffee quickly and go back and see, or should I stay here and hopefully have a conversation with that woman? In the end, her phone rings and she starts having a lively conversation with someone. Boyfriend most probably. So I finish my coffee and croissant and walk back outside and go the short distance up the road to the entrance to the office building. I go inside and check the answering machine. Sadly, there's nothing.

Then a miracle happens. The phone starts ringing. I just stand there a moment feeling like a fool. Then I pick it up. "Hello," I say, with more confidence in my voice than I actually feel.

Your reworked version:

2. Rework one of your scenes or passages

Look through the scenes and sketches you've already written and find one or two that seem to be heavy on the telling. Rework them to do more showing.

Reminder: To show rather than tell, cut filter words, reduce emotion-explaining words, use concrete rather than abstract language, use body language and actions, use dialogue, and clean up info dumps.

3. Write a new scene

This course is all about supporting you in building a story as you learn the skills of fiction-writing. By now you will have a collection of scenes and sketches, some of which might clearly be part of a single developing story and others which might seem to be random pieces that don't fit anywhere. For this exercise:

- Write a new scene or sketch for your work in progress and fine-tune it for showing vs telling, or
- If you don't yet have a story you're working on, see if any of the apparently random scenes you've already written can be further developed, or
- If you have some sketches featuring a character that intrigues you – write more about this character.

Your new scene or sketch (with more showing than telling):

Describing Settings and Characters

Description adds the magic that makes your story-world come alive. It's the words, phrases and paragraphs that give your readers a sense of place, mood, action and character. Good description evokes vivid pictures in the reader's imagination, drawing them in and making them participants in the creation of every scene.

For some reason, writers tend to either avoid description altogether or go totally overboard with it. And perhaps it's not surprising – writing good descriptive passages is an art. It's easy to mess up description by providing too much and boring the reader or being so minimalistic the writing feels bland and generic. Description is a subject that could take a whole book to cover adequately, so we'll just touch on some of the basics here. You'll find that just a little knowledge of the do's and don'ts of description will go a long way to making your writing more vivid and engaging while keeping your story moving along at a good pace.

Descriptive text is everything from a single clarifying word (e.g., 'red', 'quickly') to whole paragraphs devoted to the appearance and sensory details of a setting or other feature of the story-world. I'll begin by outlining some of the principles of description and then apply these principles to describing setting and character.

Principle 1: Use simile and metaphor

Simile and metaphor are types of comparison you can use to bring creative imagery into your descriptions. Simile makes a comparison by stating that one thing is *like* another thing. Metaphor makes a comparison by stating that one thing *is* another thing.

Simile: She's like an angel.

Metaphor: She's an angel.

As you can see, simile and metaphor perform essentially the same role – it's just that metaphor is more direct in its comparison. It requires the reader to think metaphorically. If you interpret the statement 'Gloria is an angel' literally you're going to think she's died and gone to heaven, when all you want to say is that Gloria is sweet and kind, just like an angel.

Note that sometimes the word 'metaphor' is used loosely to include simile as well. Simile is really just a form of metaphoric (i.e., non-literal) language. In this course, when I refer to metaphor, I will usually be including simile as well.

Metaphor and simile are useful when you want to describe an essential characteristic of someone or something in a fresh way.

> The clouds lay like besieging battleships on the horizon.

> "The test was pure murder," he said.

> Jordan was a peacock before a captive crowd of hens.

> She was thin, sharp and bitter. Like a needle.

> He's a total dick.

The pitfalls of metaphor

Use metaphor, but use it with care. It's very easy to overdo it and end up with something that just sounds silly. For instance, here's one that I found not so long ago:

> His thoughts bounced around in his head like rubber balls.

Do thoughts really do anything like that? Even metaphorically. The metaphor draws attention to itself rather than supporting the description. The moral of the story is to use metaphoric language but to use it with restraint. If in doubt about a metaphor, it's probably wise to let the doubt win.

Principle 2: Avoid filter words

Filter words are unnecessary words that separate the reader from the story's action. They remind us that the story is being *told* by someone rather than being experienced, or *shown*, through the eyes of the character. Examples include 'see', 'hear', 'think', 'touch', 'wonder', 'seems', 'decide', 'feel', 'know', 'watch'.

We filter the experience by saying that we 'saw' something or 'felt' something or 'thought' something. If this is sounding familiar, it should – you encountered filter words in the previous chapter on showing vs telling. You'll find that the principles of showing vs telling also apply to description. In the following examples, the first sentence contains filtering, while the second sentence has been reworked to reduce it:

Mary *felt* a sinking feeling in the pit of her stomach when she *saw* the open door.
Mary's stomach sank when she saw the open door.

*

When he *saw* that the coast was clear, he made a run for it.
When the coast was clear, he made a run for it.

*

She walked toward the orchard, *smelling* the odour of rotting fruit from a distance.
She walked toward the orchard, the odour of rotten fruit lying heavy in the air.

*

Joe *realised* he needed to come clean about his past. He *wondered* how she would take it.
Joe dreaded telling Angie about his past. How would she take it?

*

Angie looked at Joe. This is going to be terrible, she *thought*. She *knew* that dodgy look in his eyes; it *meant* he was hiding something.

Angie looked at Joe. Whatever he said it would be terrible. That dodgy look in his eyes said everything.

*

As I crested the summit, I could *feel* the icy blast tearing at my flimsy jacket and *thought* it would push me off balance if it got any stronger.

As I crested the summit, the icy blast tore at my flimsy jacket. If it got any stronger it would push me off balance.

From these examples, you can see that it's really not necessary to always filter the experience. You simply don't need to say that the character thought something or felt something if you can go directly to the experience itself. Sometimes you have to rework the sentence a bit, but you'll usually end up with something that's stronger than the filtered sentence.

Exceptions to the rule

Sometimes, no matter how hard you try, a sentence will just not work without a filter word. Here's one:

I pick up the envelope and *notice* the address is written in child's handwriting.

I can try rewriting it like this:

I pick up the envelope. The address is written in child's handwriting.

I've eliminated the filter word but I'm not so sure the sentence is really any better. It's a bit clunky now. In this case, it might be better to keep the filter word.

Filter words are also used legitimately when they are important to the meaning of the sentence. For instance, it might be important to know what the character hears or sees:

Mary's stomach sank when she *saw* the open door.

We *heard* the bombers before we saw them.

We *watched* them grow up; they were part of our family.

"I *know* you don't mean it, Joe."

In summary, pay attention to filter words and see if you really need them. Can you find a way to state the experience directly? If so, cut the filter word and rework the sentence. If not, leave the filter word where it is.

Principle 3: Reduce adverbs and adjectives

There is a good piece of writing advice that goes: 'Write with nouns and verbs, not with adjectives and adverbs.'

Adverbs

Adverbs are words that tell you more about verbs, for example, 'She spoke *softly*'. Adverbs are the main ones to be wary of because they are something agents and publishers tend to look out for as an indicator of weak prose. Many adverbs end in -ly, so it's quite easy to recognise them. Some agents or publishers will just scan a few pages and if they see too many -ly words they'll put the manuscript down and won't read further.

So what's the problem with adverbs?

Well, it's mainly because they indicate the presence of weak verbs. Weak verbs are imprecise verbs that rely on adverbs for their meaning. In these examples, the verbs and their adverbs are in italics:

He *ran quickly* out the door.

She *looked* at him *menacingly*.

He *touched* her *clumsily*.

She *hastily entered* the room and confronted Harold.

Now we'll try these sentences using strong verbs instead. Strong verbs can stand on their own without adverbs. They are precise in their meaning.

He *dashed* out the door.

She *glared* at him.

He *groped* her.

She *burst* into the room and confronted Harold.

You can probably see that the sentences using strong verbs are more alive and intense. Weak verbs tend to be overused and end up making the writing tepid and imprecise. Think of 'ran quickly'. You would only write that if you were too rushed to find a more accurate verb, of which there are plenty (galloped, sprinted, raced, darted, hurried, hurtled, sped, whizzed, zoomed, zipped, charged, flew...).

Another place where unnecessary adverbs pop up consistently is in dialogue tags. We've already made this point in the dialogue section but it's worth repeating here. Generally, you should avoid adding an adverb to the 'he/she said' speech tag, for example:

"Come here at once," he said *menacingly*.

It should be clear from what's happening in the scene that the speaker is being menacing, so stating that he is speaking menacingly amounts to over-description. The only exception is when there isn't any clue in the text to indicate the speaker's tone, for instance:

"Come here at once," she said *softly*.

You need 'softly' there because one would expect this kind of statement to be delivered with a loud voice or particular intensity. The softness is unexpected so needs to be made explicit.

Adjectives

Adjectives tell us more about nouns and pronouns. For example, 'I was *delighted* by your gift.' The adjective 'delighted' tells you more about my state of being.

So far so good. The problem comes in when we overuse adjectives that don't hold much meaning. For instance, the following adjectives tend to be overused while also being generic and imprecise: 'beautiful', 'interesting', 'lovely', 'exciting', 'nice', 'big', 'sad'.

We had such an interesting day. (How vague and bland)

This *huge* dog chased me. (So vague I'm not feeling at all scared.)

Jess felt *sad* at the thought Tom would leave her. (Just sad? Not perhaps grief, agony, mournfulness, or wretchedness?)

With adjectives, first check whether you need them. Have you just sprinkled them into the text because they sound nice but don't really say anything? If so, dump them. Then check whether the adjectives that remain are strong and precise. Drop the vague ones and replace them with adjectives that do some real work. Let's do a final example. This one uses a vague and squishy adjective and a weak verb-adverb combination.

The *big* dog barked *angrily*.

Not very threatening, is it? I'll try some stronger descriptive words and see if we can turn up the volume a bit:

The foam-jawed beast of a Rottweiler threw itself into a spasm of barking and snapping.

Principle 4: Add sensory details

When we think of description we tend to focus on visual appearance. However, to really draw readers into the story-world, we need to appeal to all their senses so they not only see it but feel it, hear it, smell it and taste it. Naturally, you don't want to throw in all the senses in every description as that would be overdoing it, but where appropriate, see if you can move beyond just the visual impression.

These examples show more than one sense being evoked:

The orchard shimmered in the midday heat and the sickly sweet scent of rotting fruit lay heavy in the air.

I lay awake to the dull drone of the neighbour's air conditioner and the cloying odour of frying oil wafting up from the all-night takeaway downstairs.

*

The balmy summer air was laced with the scent of pool chlorine and coconut oil.

Here are some sensory words you can use to spice up your descriptions:

- Sight: gloomy, dazzling, foggy, smeared, watery, brilliant, lucid
- Touch: rough, smooth, grainy, gritty, prickly, viscous, fluffy, sharp, needling
- Hearing: thumping, bass, treble, squeaky, tinny, echoing, reverberating, soaring
- Taste and smell: rancid, sour, sweet, pungent, thin, cloying, suffocating, sweet, honeyed
- Motion: zipping, racing, leaden, soaring, fleeting, diving, galloping, trembling, quivering, shivering, swooping

Beware of over-describing

Just as it's possible to be too bland and vague in your descriptions, it's possible to go overboard and end up with overly ornate and wordy prose (also known as purple prose) or images and metaphors that just sound off.

Her nose quivered with the smell of rotting fruit.

Unless she's a horse, her nose isn't going to quiver. This is an example of trying to be too creative in coming up with descriptions.

Principle 5: Describe characters and events in motion

When you sit down to describe a character or a setting, you'll probably find yourself sketching out a list of qualities that describe that object. And that's fine as a first draft to help you get clear on the important features. What you want to avoid, however, is just dumping that list into your text as a blob of description that is separate from the action.

For instance, suppose you imagine a character called Melissa who looks a bit like a Barbie doll. As you see her in your mind's eye she's got wavy, gold hair, big blue eyes, and cupid lips. So in your story you write:

> Melissa had long, wavy gold hair and big, blue eyes and a smile that could make Cupid blush.

So apart from being a bit clichéd, it's also kind of boring. The problem is that the description is static and it's pure telling rather than showing. In general, a better way to describe anything in your story is to describe it *in motion* – in other words, as part of the unfolding experience of action and events. You weave the description into the narrative so that it sounds more natural and doesn't stand awkward and alone.

> Melissa flicked her long, gold hair and gave me a coy look with her big, blue eyes. "Well, aren't you the gentleman," she said, then pursed her cupid lips in a mock kiss.

In this passage, you get the full description of her without it feeling like you're being described to. You're not being told what she's like, you're actually experiencing it together with the narrator as the story is unfolding. I'll give some more examples in the discussion on setting and character below.

But before we get there, a brief word about the exceptions. In writing, as you're coming to discover, every guideline can be overturned if you have a good cause to do so. For instance, as I was writing the first Melissa example, a second sentence popped out that took things in a new direction:

> Melissa had long, wavy gold hair and big, blue eyes and a smile that could make Cupid blush. We used to think her heart must have been made of gold, too, but then the thing happened that showed us otherwise.

The second sentence comes as a surprise precisely because it contrasts with the first sentence. The Barbie doll facade is built up in the first sentence and is broken with the second, creating a tantalising hook. So by all means write discrete descriptive passages if they serve your purpose.

Describing setting

The setting is the space in which an action happens. You need to give your readers a sense of the features of this space so they have a context for the action and can build a more vivid picture of it. Traditionally, authors would spend some time sketching the setting before the action began. But nowadays, readers have shorter attention spans and they want to get to the action quicker.

So that leaves us with a bit of a conundrum. How do we describe setting in a way that gives readers enough information to create a mental image of the scene but without boring them at the same time? One answer is that you begin with just enough description to get the action going, and then you weave the rest of the description into the action as it's happening. In other words, you describe things in motion.

For instance, suppose we have a scene where two figures are trudging up a hill to a castle. We could start the scene with a static or isolated description of the setting:

> The castle stood grey and forbidding on a hill covered with shards of black rock and small tufts of heather and moss. An icy wind blew down from the snow-capped peaks of Mount Arack, a day's ride to the north. It was silent except for the eerie sighing of wind through the castle's turrets and spires. Gregory and Father Anselm trudged up the hill path towards the castle.

There's nothing particularly wrong with that description – it's just a bit static and, well, bland. A bit too much like a list of characteristics. So, let's see what happens if we weave the description into the actions of the characters:

> Gregory and Father Anselm trudged up the hill path, taking care not to slip on the treacherous shards of wet rock that slithered down from the slopes above them. The boy stood to catch his breath and looked up at the castle. It loomed over them – grey, forbidding and silent but for the sighing of wind through its turrets and spires. "Come on," said Father Anselm, leaning on his staff. "There'll be a fire in the great hall. And warm food."
>
> Gregory said nothing but pulled his cloak tighter around him as an icy gust blew down from distant

Mount Arack. The snow-capped peaks of the mountain lay in a shifting, watery light that brought no warmth but spoke only of a dark yet to come.

In this passage, the setting is described in motion – it unfolds as the characters experience it. Sensory details of colour, mood and texture are added to the narrative action without slowing it down unnecessarily. And there are no filter words distancing the reader from the experience. But more than this – the gloom of the landscape becomes a metaphor for Gregory's inner state, giving us a sense of how he is feeling as he trudges towards the castle. And the last phrase – 'spoke only of a dark yet to come' – foreshadows trouble ahead. The setting description here is not just listing characteristics of the landscape, it's doing the work of telling the story. The description carries meaning and movement.

The whole effect is more intense than the static description in the first example and more true to how we really experience settings – as sensory experiences unfolding with action and motion.

Pro tip: Avoid starting a story with long passages of description that have the sole purpose of building your story-world. Fantasy and sci-fi writers, particularly, have a love of world-building and can easily fall into the trap of creating static opening sequences where nothing much happens. Landscapes and fantastical worlds only become interesting when things happen in them. So start with the happening and then sketch in the details of the world as you go along.

Describing characters

The lazy way of describing someone is to simply list their characteristics.

> Mac was six-foot-five, had huge, muscled arms and big black eyebrows that met at the middle. Everybody was afraid of him until they got to know him.

So far so boring. To really make this character come alive you need to haul out your toolbox of descriptive language and get to work. So begin asking yourself questions like these:

- How can I demonstrate/show his appearance rather than tell it?
- What creative comparisons come to mind, i.e., what metaphors and similes might help paint a picture of his size?
- How can I describe him in motion rather than through static description?

Let's try this out. I'm thinking of a huge man and how I could describe him in motion using more showing than telling. I get the image of him walking into a bar and having to stoop because he's so tall.

> Mac lumbered into the bar, ducking his head where it almost got clipped by the ceiling fan. He pulled up two stools and sat down on both of them then ordered a Corona draught and a plate of fries. People looked at him in the half-stunned, half-guilty way they looked at car wrecks and things that were born that shouldn't have been. That's the effect Big Mac had on people, at least till they got to know him a bit. The barman slid the frothing draft to him and he nodded a thanks and took the great

beer mug like a thimble in his paw and drained half of it in one long slug.

This description starts with him in motion – he 'lumbers' into a bar and ducks his head to avoid getting clipped by the ceiling fan. This is also showing his size rather than telling. Then he takes up two stools at the bar, which is more demonstration and showing (yes, slightly exaggerated, but what the hell). The description then shifts to look at him through the eyes of others, showing us how they see him. People stare at him like he's some kind of freak. The last sentence uses a simile (the beer mug being like a thimble) and a metaphor (his hand is a paw) to give a visual sense of his bear-like size.

That description is in third-person omniscient with an abstract narrator. Let's try a different scene with a first-person narrator describing the same big fellow:

Mac was big. Not just any big – dump-truck big. No kidding. By the age of 13 he was playing first-team football with guys who were already growing beards. And he just kept on growing from there. His favourite party trick was to pull a one-ton pickup with a rope clamped in his teeth. He'd tow it all the way up the road and then untie the rope and fix it to the trailer hitch and drag the damn truck all the way back. You wouldn't want to pick a fight with Big Mac Deschamps, no sir. Even if he called your mother a ho, you'd just shut right up and walk on by. Hell, even on a good day a hug from him could kill you.

This passage describes Big Mac in motion using a series of stories – first about his football playing and then about him pulling a truck with his teeth. The narrator does some telling –

he says straight out that Mac is big, but then he goes on and embellishes it with a simile (dump-truck big) and plenty of showing. What really makes this description come alive is the narrator's voice – you get a sense of a real person with characteristic turns of phrase and colourful expression.

Describing a first-person narrator

In third-person omniscient narration it's quite easy to describe your protagonist because you've got an abstract viewpoint from which to do so. But what happens if your narration is first-person and you want to describe the protagonist, the 'I' narrator?

Some writers allow their 'I' narrators to describe themselves, but then you end up with statements like:

> I'm six foot tall, have warm, brown eyes and an infectious sense of humour.

That just sounds false. We never really describe ourselves like this, so it doesn't work in fiction. If you really need to describe your first-person protagonist, get another character to comment on their appearance.

> "Oh darling," said Mother, giving me an up and down glance, "you've gone and put all that bounce back on your hips."

Or give the reader clues in the thoughts and actions of the protagonist. For instance, if they are overweight, let them get on a scale, look at the number, and then dash to the kitchen to binge-eat half a packet of biscuits. That will tell the reader all they need to know about the character's weight issue.

Something else to consider is that you don't really need to tell the reader exact details about the narrator's appearance. Does the audience really need to know that the heroine's hair is dark and her eyes are green? What if the reader has another idea of beauty and prefers her heroine to be blonde and blue-eyed? Unless it's really important, don't feel you have to tell the reader anything about the narrator's appearance. If, for the purposes of your story, it's important that she has green eyes because this indicates she's got elven blood, have another character remark on the colour of her eyes. Use your skills of showing vs telling to plant information in dialogue, comments and actions.

And whatever you do – never be tempted to put your 'I' narrator in front of a mirror and have them describe their reflection. This tactic has been done to death and is totally unrealistic. Do you ever stand in front of a mirror and describe yourself? Just don't.

Description and point of view

What you can describe, and how you describe it, will be influenced by the point of view in which your story is told.

First-person

In first-person, I, you can only describe what the focal character sees and experiences. You can't describe a setting if the character is not there witnessing it for themselves. You can also not describe it using a voice other than the focal character's. For instance, if your character is a sassy young woman with a bright personality, your setting descriptions will have to be in her voice. You can't use vocabulary or tone she wouldn't use. If the day is overcast and threatening rain, don't describe the clouds hulking like battleships above the black shards of Mount Doom. Have her say something like, "Rain. Darn it! There goes our picnic."

Third-person limited

This is written in the grammatical third-person (he, she, it) and tells the story through the eyes of a particular character. It's like first-person where you can only show what the character sees, just written in third-person. There is some leeway with third limited, however, so you can pull back a bit from the character and you don't have to narrate exactly in their voice. For instance, you can say something like:

> When Patty Pep woke on Saturday morning she looked out the window and saw the storm gathering above Mount Doom. Clouds lay heavy and dark on the black slopes of the old volcano and lightning flashed above its crown. Oh no, thought Patty. There goes our picnic.

The description of the storm is not in Patty's voice but it is tied to her viewpoint. It only describes what she can see. And while the description is not exactly in her voice, it is also not too far from it. If it got any more poetic or serious it would contrast too much with her peppy voice and the reader would sense a discord.

Third-person omniscient

Omniscient point of view is written in grammatical third-person and uses an abstract narrator, i.e., the narrator is not an actual character in the story. Omniscient narration is thought of as god-like – the narrator can see everything and be any-where and know everything that has ever happened or is going to happen. Because the narrator is not tied to a character's par-ticular view of the situation you are free to describe anything you like. You can also pass judgement on the characters or comment on what is about to happen.

> When Patty Pep woke on Saturday morning she looked out the window and saw a storm gathering above Mount Doom. Clouds lay heavy and dark on the black slopes of the old volcano and lightning flashed above its crown. Out of sight within the old crater, a jagged fis-sure lurched open, spewing gobs of red lava and a sulphurous mist from which emerged the hideous forms of a thousand animated corpses. Satan's Fifth Le-gion! Their sleep of a thousand years was over and mayhem was about to be let loose into the world. Back at the ranch, Patty stared glumly at the approaching rain and the flashes of light from the mountain. Oh, darn, she thought. There goes our picnic.

Mistakes with setting and description

Over-describing

How much is too much? Well, that's always going to be subjec-tive, and a lot also depends on the genre you're writing in. But generally, it's a good idea to be very selective with the descrip-tive details and share only what is necessary to give an idea of the setting or the character. Readers who enjoy a fast pace often skip over lengthy descriptions if they don't seem essential to the story.

Remember that fiction is predominantly a narrative mode of writing, so you don't want your description to dominate. If it does, you're writing a poem rather than a story.

Purple prose

This is a type of over-describing that happens when we try too hard to make our writing interesting and end up resorting to cliché and overly ornate or poetic language.

Her eyes were limpid pools of azure.

Her dark locks cascaded down her shoulders like a flock of descending ravens.

Let's examine that last one. For starters, 'cascading locks' is clichéd – it's been done a zillion times. And the simile 'like a flock of descending ravens' is certainly creative but does long black hair really look anything like a flock of ravens? Not really. The metaphor stretches things just a bit too far and draws attention to itself rather than to the subject being described.

Telling

The principle of 'show don't tell' applies to description just as much as it applies to any other kind of writing you'll produce as you build your story. For instance, if you want to describe a peaceful neighbourhood street, try not to resort to using the word 'peaceful'. Just stock it with picket fences, friendly Labradors and kids on bicycles.

If it's a violent street, give it rusty wire fences, shifty-eyed boys lounging at the corner, and snarling Rottweilers on chains. Throw in the sound of a police siren in the distance and some hip-hop pounding from a slowly cruising Buick and your scene will be complete.

Summary

The main ideas from this chapter:

- Use simile and metaphor: Simile and metaphor are types of comparison you can use to bring creative imagery into your descriptions.
- Avoid filter words: Filter words are unnecessary words that separate the reader from the story's action, e.g., 'thought', 'saw', 'felt'.
- Reduce your use of adverbs and adjectives: Instead, use strong verbs and precise nouns.
- Add sensory details: Don't just describe how something looks – see if you can add other senses such as smell, sound, touch and taste.
- Describe characters and scenes in motion: Try weaving description into the action so it's not separate from the narrative.
- Pay attention to the limits of point of view: You can only describe what your narrator can see, hear or feel.
- Avoid over-describing, purple prose, and too much telling.

Exercises

1. Write a descriptive passage

Write a short descriptive passage involving a character and a setting. Use the descriptive language tools you learned in this chapter.

Length: A paragraph or two. See the examples used in this module, for example, the Big Mac and the Father Anselm sketches. Your sketch doesn't need to be longer than these, though it can be. Don't think too hard about it. Freewrite on any character, landscape or setting that comes to mind. When you've found something workable, spend some time polishing it and making it into a mini-scene with action, dialogue and description.

Subject: Write on one of the story ideas you are working on for this course. Or try something completely new. Here are some writing prompts if you need ideas to get you started:

- Travellers approach a castle/town/fortress/cave.
- A woman meets a man she instantly dislikes, though he will soon become her lover (change genders if necessary).
- A boy or girl is brought to a room where someone gives them important information.
- Someone is lying (without telling us directly that he's lying).
- Someone walks through a park or down a street and feels they are being followed.
- The setting of a battle that is about to begin (or the aftermath of a battle).
- Someone arrives home and finds something disturbing.

- Someone walks through an apocalyptic landscape looking for something.

2. Improve a passage from your work-in-progress

Look at the scenes you've already written for your story or portfolio and identify one that could do with some improved description. Rework the description so it is more powerful and immediate. This can be as simple as moving some static description into the action so it is description 'in motion' or adding few words of sensory detail to a passage.

PART 3

Story completion

In Part 1 of this course, you were introduced to story structure and gained insight into how to define a premise that gets a story going. And in Part 2, you were shown some of the key writing techniques that will enable you to tell that story in more masterful prose. Now it's time to return to the subject of story and plot structure so you can build the middle and end parts of your stories.

CHAPTER 11

Building Your Story with Scenes

Once you've got a premise for your story, or at least a promising story idea, it's time to start developing the story and giving it shape. As you do this, you will start working with the basic building block of structure – the scene.

You can think of scenes as micro-stories within your greater story. They have a beginning, middle and end, even if very brief. And they have some kind of action, which can be as simple as a conversation or as complex as a car chase. A description of a landscape is not a scene, but a description of someone walking through that landscape to meet somebody is.

We can say that a scene is a section of a story made up of a character (or characters) performing some kind of action that drives the plot or develops the theme. A great story is a collection of well-structured and purposeful scenes that flow smoothly from one to the other.

A new scene usually starts whenever you change one or more of the following:
- Character: When you start following a different character or change the character through whose eyes the story is being told.
- Location: If characters move from one house to another, that's a new scene. If they move from inside a room to outside the same room, that's probably a new scene, especially if the subject of conversation changes.
- Time period: If the characters do something in the morning and then something else in the afternoon, that should probably be two scenes.
- Plot point: Plot points are major turning points of the story, for example, the opening scene, the climax, and the resolution. You'll learn more about these in the chapter on basic story structure.

You might be wondering if it's really important to know all this about when a scene starts and ends, but knowing this can help you avoid the mistake of chopping and changing between scenes too quickly. Without being consciously aware of it, we have become used to extremely rapid scene changes through watching movies and TV series. A single minute of film might race us through four scene changes without causing any confusion. It works because the viewer has an immediate visual cue that the scene has changed and they know exactly where they are. But in writing, you need to give readers a bit more time to process location and character changes. That's why you need to start thinking in terms of scenes as being micro-stories rather than as story fragments (unless you're writing a screenplay).

The purpose of a scene

We've said that every scene should have some kind of action that advances the story in some way. This means that every scene has a purpose. Here are some common scene purposes:

1. Build suspense
2. Introduce or develop characters
3. Develop theme (the philosophy or message underlying the work)
4. Establish mood and setting
5. Give backstory
6. Introduce or intensify conflict
7. Show clues or red herrings (misleading clues)
8. Reflect, regroup and decide on new action

Here are some made-up examples of scenes and purposes. Note how the scene changes whenever location or character changes.

The airport

Scene 1: A husband waits for his wife at airport arrivals. They greet and have a friendly catch-up conversation while walking to the car (*Purpose: Move the story forward, introduce characters*).

Scene 2: In the car on the way home they have a fight (*Purpose: Reveal tensions in the marriage, intensify conflict*).

Scene 3: Back home, the husband retreats to his den, pours himself a stiff drink and sends a text message to his secretary (*Purpose: reflecting on what happened and deciding on new action*).

Scene 4: The wife sits alone at her dressing table. She slips her wedding ring off and puts it in a jewellery box (*Purpose: reflecting on events and choosing a new direction*).

*

The castle

Scene 1: A figure walks through a fantasy landscape towards a dark castle in the distance. The character bangs on the castle door and gives a password when challenged by the guards (*Purpose: Establish the setting and introduce character*).

Scene 2: He enters, states his name (Gregory of Winchester), and says he has an important message for Lord Boltar. He is escorted to the lord's chambers (*Purpose: Establish setting [the castle], establish character, move the story forward*).

Scene 3: Gregory meets with Lord Boltar and delivers his message. Boltar reacts violently and begins interrogating Gregory on the contents of the message. Then he orders his guards to arrest him (*Purpose: Introduce character, intensify conflict, give backstory*).

Tip: As you write you'll be churning out a large number of scenes, but a fair number of them will end up being merely exploratory or experimental and won't have a useful purpose in your story. This is where you need to get a bit ruthless and do some trimming. Only include those scenes that really do have a purpose that drives the story forward or that deepens it in some way. A simple test: If the scene can be deleted and it doesn't change the story in any meaningful way, consider deleting it.

Scene openings

It seems logical that you should start each scene with a little bit of introductory information about which character we are following, where they are, and how they got there. But if you start each scene this way it can get quite monotonous. It's also not always the most engaging way to begin. You can make your writing more immediate and immersive by exploring different ways of beginning. You have four choices for how to open your scene:

- Description
- Dialogue
- Thought
- Action

Let's make up some examples.

David sat on the park bench and stared morosely at his phone. He wondered whether she really had forgotten about their date or whether he'd just plain been stood up.

That's not a bad scene intro, but it's just one way to start. You could get more immediacy by swinging it around to begin with the thought:

She's forgotten. I can't frickin believe it! David sat on the park bench and stared at the empty screen of his phone. Or I've been stood up. Typical!

That feels a bit more immediate. It prompts questions in the reader's mind (Who has forgotten? What have they forgotten? Who is speaking?) The questions are answered almost immediately, but they are enough to hook the reader and grab their interest.

When you begin a scene in the middle of an action or a dialogue it's called beginning *in medias res*. It means, literally, in the middle of things.

> "You bastard!"
>
> "What?"
>
> "You know damn well," said Alyssa, shoving a scrap of newspaper at me.
>
> I took the paper and read the headline. "It wasn't my idea," I said softly. "They put me up to it. Andy and Bob. It's their—"
>
> "Oh, you're all such idiots!"

When the scene starts in the dialogue above, the reader doesn't know who is speaking, but they'll be hooked by the energy of the statement and by the questions it poses: Who is speaking, who is the bastard, and what did they do? All the required information will become clear as the scene develops. The questions are hooks that compel the reader to read on. Also notice how this approach cuts out all extra fluff and explanations that get in the way of direct action. The effect is one of immediacy and aliveness. You also get free rein to cut out all those boring 'hello, how are you?' dialogue openings. The reader doesn't need that detail – just throw them into the action and let them sink or swim.

Tip: Begin some of your scenes *in medias res*. It will electrify your writing and free you from the habit of over-explaining things. Let the reader get involved in figuring out what's going on.

Scene structure and flow

If you look at common scene purposes listed earlier, you'll probably notice that scenes can do wildly different jobs. Some are full of action and big events while others are quieter and more reflective. Scenes tend to flow in a natural cycle of active and reactive moments. For instance, if one scene describes a battle, the next will show the aftermath and consequences.

Technically, these are called action scenes and sequel scenes, or just 'scene and sequel'. Action and sequel scenes have a structure that goes something like this:

Action scene: The character has a *goal*, encounters *opposition*, and *succeeds* or *fails*.

Sequel scene: Character feels *emotion* about the outcome, *thinks* about it, *decides* on a new goal, and begins taking *action* (which becomes the goal of the next scene).

You can simplify it to this: The character pursues a goal and succeeds or fails (action scene). Then they reflect on the outcome and devise a new plan with a new goal (sequel), leading to a new action scene.

Suppose Joe has been growing a bit paunchy of late, so his wife, Beth, puts him on a strict diet. Joe manages to stick to the diet in the daytime, but at night he gets hit with cravings. Here's a plan for the scenes that might unfold from the situation:

Action scene

Joe wakes up in the middle of the night with stomach rumbling. The image of that leftover piece of sausage in the refrigerator is too much to resist (*Goal*). Not wanting to wake Beth, he tiptoes downstairs without switching the lights on. As he approaches the kitchen he trips over the sleeping dog, who jumps up and howls. Joe gets a fright and falls back into the furniture, toppling a vase that smashes on the floor (*Opposition*). At this point, Beth wakes up and thinks they are being burgled, so she trips the panic alarm. Lights come on in the windows of their neighbours (*Failure*).

Sequel scene

Joe sits in the dark with chaos all around him. That'll serve you right, he chides himself (*Emotion*). He wonders (*Thought*) whether there's still time to dive into the refrigerator and bolt down that piece of sausage. Or perhaps he should admit the truth about his midnight snacking. He decides to tell Beth that he came downstairs to investigate a strange sound (*Decision*). He pats the dog and walks back to the staircase (*Action*).

The action becomes the goal of the next scene. In this case, to go back to his room to tell his wife the lie about what he was doing downstairs.

You might be wondering whether this sequel really is a distinct scene or just the reflective ending of a scene, and I'd say it's the latter. The whole sequence with Joe sneaking downstairs, getting into trouble, and going back upstairs is one scene. The name 'scene and sequel' can lead to a bit of confusion because it implies that the sequel is a separate scene, when quite often it's not (see the 'Murder Mystery' example on the next page for more clarification on this subject).

Why is it useful to know all this about action and sequel scenes?

- Because it gives you a way of pacing your story so that you don't just have one action flowing into the next and the next without pause.
- It helps you build your story by giving you clues as to what to say next: If you've written an action scene or two, follow it with a sequel scene (or just a sequel passage) that takes us to the emotional level and reconnects with the character's inner journey.
- It can help you unclutter your scenes by separating action from reflection (See the example scene below).

Scene and sequel example: 'Murder mystery'

Here's a scene I wrote for this exercise. I chose to jump straight in with sensory detail and dialogue, leaving out explanation of motives and feelings so as not to dilute the immediacy of the moment. The emotional content and more of the backstory is given in the last paragraph, which is the sequel passage to the action scene.

Scene plan

Location: A woodland somewhere in rural England

Character: Detective Sergeant Sherwood

Purpose: Introduce character, initiate murder mystery, introduce backstory

Opening scene

First they tied him to a tree with his arms stretched back around the trunk and the wrists bound with cable ties. Then they went to work on him. Something like a cheese grater or a wood rasp, judging from the ragged strips of ripped flesh on his face and chest. I took a step back from the corpse and held the back of my hand to my nose. Early morning mist hung in the dreary woodland, the scent of wet earth and leaves struck through with the odour of rot. A constable cordoned off the area with yellow and blue tape while a forensics officer zipped himself into a sterile bodysuit.

I heard a sound behind me and turned and saw a grey-haired man walking up from the dirt path, pulling on rubber gloves as he walked. DCI Penny, I assumed. He stopped next to me and peered at the body and grimaced. Then he looked at me. "And who are you?" he said.

"DS Sherwood. Transferred from Birmingham yesterday."

"It just follows you wherever you go, doesn't it?"

"Sir?"

"The stench of death. Of evil. You think you're leaving the city for a quiet life in the country but it finds you anyway."

"I wasn't ... well, I mean, I came because of the wife, see. She doesn't do well in the city. And my boy. He ran into some bad company back home. I mean, back there."

The chief inspector turned abruptly from me and took a step closer to the corpse. "What do you see, DS Sherwood?" he said, leaning over the body, unaffected by the cloying smell.

"Torture, Sir."

"And what more?"

"Well, I'd say it's a message of some kind. Bit too elaborate for the benefit of its recipient alone, if you know what I mean."

DCI Penny looked at the corpse grimly and nodded. "That looks about right," he said. Then he stood back, gave me a steely eyed nod, and walked back to the woodland track without another word.

He'd guessed right about me leaving the city for a quiet life in the country. That had been the plan anyway. Just routine burglaries and vandalism, they'd said. Nothing more than the usual antisocial behaviour and some rowdiness around the pubs on a Friday night. But as I stood looking at that corpse I knew the promise had been a lie. Death and trouble had followed me. I wouldn't tell Emily. Not just yet, anyway.

In this example, the last paragraph ('He'd guessed right about me leaving the city ...') is the sequel passage. Notice how the mood changes to become more reflective, allowing us access to Sherwood's thoughts and giving opportunity for filling in the backstory about how he was looking for a quiet life in the country. Also note that it's not really a separate scene as neither character, time nor location change – it's more like a reflective passage that is the sequel to the action passage. Together they make up one complete scene.

The important thing at this stage is not to get too hung up on the technicalities – I've only introduced this subject because it gives us a handy way to organise the narration into separate active and reflective passages. Of course, you don't always have to separate things like this, but it can help to make scenes more dramatic by moving backstory and reflections out of the action passage where they might be slowing things down.

Troubleshooter: Mixed scene and sequel

Are your action scenes being slowed down by explanations, emotions and backstory? Consider cutting out most of the explanations and emotional content and putting them in a reflective sequel passage. That way, you unclutter your scenes and give each one a clearer purpose.

How to indicate scene breaks

In printed works, you usually need some kind of typographic (text layout and formatting) indicator that lets the reader know they are entering a new scene. The simplest way of doing this is to leave a slightly larger paragraph break and to start the first line of the new scene flush with the margin instead of indented.

To give a stronger break, you can add a text ornament in the space between scenes. Some fonts in your word processing program have special ornaments you can use, but the simplest is just to add three centred asterisks. In the example below, a strong scene break is indicated by asterisks, with the first line of the new scene beginning flush with the left margin.

> Once upon a time, there was a poor widow who lived with her son, Jack, in a cottage at the edge of the village. Their only money came from selling the milk of their old cow, Bessy. But one sad day, Bessy gave no milk, so they had no money at all.

"Oh, what shall we do?" cried the widow. "We're going to die of hunger."

"I know," said Jack. "We'll have to sell Bessy. Then we can buy some seed and plant some vegetables to sell. And get some chickens to lay eggs."

"Good idea," said the widow. "Go to market tomorrow and sell Old Bessy."

***

"Hello, young Jack," said the strange-looking old man to Jack as he led Bessy down the road the next morning.

"Good morning to you," said Jack, wondering how the man knew his name.

In this example, you could also leave out the asterisks and just have the deep paragraph break. However, the scene jump is quite abrupt so there is a case for keeping the asterisks. If you have a more transitioned scene break, with the new scene flowing smoothly and logically from the first scene, you can get away with a less dramatic scene break marker.

Note that you don't need any special typographical break between action passage and sequel passage if they are part of the same scene (as in the 'Murder Mystery' example earlier).

Troubleshooter: Scene-hopping

Does your story have many characters who we follow (point-of-view characters)? If so, be careful not to jump from following one character to another with only an ordinary paragraph break between them. Remember that if we are changing point-of-view character, we are also changing scenes, so to avoid confusing your reader, you need to set off the new scene by starting a new chapter or by using typography that indicates a scene break.

Imagining and planning scenes

You'll probably find there are two ways you imagine and write your scenes – spontaneous creation and planned creation.

Spontaneous scene creation

Sometimes you don't have a fully fledged story but you do have one resonant moment full of mood or tension or questions. So you begin there, with the scene, and see what develops. Sometimes, the purpose of a scene is only revealed after you've written it. Your story might only emerge once you've written down some scenes and can see a pattern beginning to form. In this case, you can come back later and remove or update scenes that don't seem to fit the overall story that has begun to develop. You can apply the technical details later. The main thing is just to get your bolt of inspiration down on paper before it disappears.

For instance, in the 'Murder Mystery' scene I shared earlier, I began with the random thought, *A detective reflects on the biggest murder mystery of his career*. Then the image came of a body tied to a tree, and I just wrote that scene without any further planning. As I began writing, other details began surfacing that were completely unplanned. By the end of the scene, I felt I had the beginnings of what could become a decent story. The point is, I didn't write it with any purpose other than to write a short scene for this course. The actual writing revealed the purpose as a character with a backstory began to emerge and other details came forward. The moral of the story is – don't overthink it, just write it and see what happens.

Planned scene creation

Other times you'll have a strong sense of story and you'll sit down to write a planned and purposeful scene that drives the story forward. This is the approach I've emphasised with all the technical discussion in this module, but it's certainly not the only way to get your scene-machine fired up and running.

The reality is that sometimes you'll just have a scene and no clear story yet, and that's fine – write it down and see where it leads. At other times you'll know exactly what scene you've got to write next and can spend a few moments planning it. But even then, things can get out of hand very quickly as your characters take things in their own direction and spontaneous, unplanned scenes start flooding your imagination. Write down everything that comes to you and then take a step back and assess the results. Has the story gone in a new direction that you really like, or have you gone down a path that ends in an impenetrable thicket? You won't know until you've written it all down. First write, then edit and attend to the technical details.

The context of this lesson

Scenes are important as the building blocks of your story. They help you structure your text and they also give you a framework for what to write next. If you don't know how scenes work, you can end up making mistakes with point of view and making confusing jumps between viewpoint characters and settings. This introduction to scenes prepares you for the next two chapters where you'll see how scenes work as part of a plot structure.

Summary

Key points from this chapter:

- A scene is a section of a story made up of a character (or characters) performing some kind of action that drives the plot or develops the theme.
- A new scene begins whenever you change character, location, time period or plot point.
- Each scene should have a particular purpose, for example, to build suspense, to introduce characters, to give backstory, to intensify conflict, and to move the story forward.
- It's a good idea to vary the way you begin scenes. Scenes can begin with description, action, thought, or dialogue. For extra immediacy, begin *in medias res* (in the middle of the action).
- Action scenes go well with reaction or sequel scenes in which the character reflects on what just happened and decides on a new action. The sequel is often not a separate scene but merely a reflective moment at the end of a scene.
- Create a clear typographical break in the text when starting a new scene.
- Scenes can emerge spontaneously from a resonant idea or image without any clear idea for a story. Or you can begin with the story and write purposeful, planned scenes that move the story forward.

Exercises

Without being aware of it, you've been writing scenes or partial scenes in the exercises for the preceding sessions. Now you have the knowledge to flesh these out into more complete scenes or a sequence of scenes.

Write a scene

Write a complete scene. You can build on an existing sketch you've been working on for this course or try something new. Begin with a brief scene plan in which you note the location, main character and scene purpose (see the 'Murder Mystery' scene example above). Write at least a page. Write two scenes, if necessary, to fill up a page.

Tip: Sometimes you don't know the purpose of a scene before you start writing it. If that's the case, just write out the scene first and then see what purpose the scene might have if it were to form part of a bigger story. Sometimes your subconscious mind knows the purpose before your conscious mind does.

If you need some help coming up with ideas for scenes, try these scene prompts:
- A crime scene.
- Saying goodbye in an airport or station.
- Confronting a cheating partner.
- A friend reveals some information they didn't mean to.
- A setting, for example, a landscape, cityscape, room (be sure to include a character in the scene and some kind of action, even if subtle).
- Someone says 'I love you' without using those words.
- A woman finds a cardboard box on her doorstep.

- A phone next to a bed rings and wakes someone up.

Things to remember:
- Experiment with different ways of starting, e.g., with an intro description, with dialogue, or in the middle of the action.
- Experiment with scene and sequel (an action scene followed by a reflective passage, possibly leading into the next action).
- Use freewriting if you get stuck.
- Don't aim for perfection. Allow yourself to write an imperfect and experimental scene.

CHAPTER 12

Structuring Your Story

In the previous chapter you were introduced to scenes as the basic building block of story structure. Now we'll take it further and explore how those building blocks fit together into an overarching structure for your whole story.

But first, a question: Are you a plotter or a pantser?

Believe it or not, this is a serious question in the writing world, so let's take a moment to think about it. A plotter is someone who loves to plot out their story structure in great detail before beginning any writing work. And a pantser is one who likes to fly by the seat of their pants – just sitting down and writing and trusting that they'll get where they need to go in the end. While these seem to be completely opposite approaches, they actually work well together.

Pantsers will usually write out their whole story without much of a thought about the premise, plot and other structural elements. Their aim is to get their ideas down as quickly as possible and then see what plot emerges. This approach is perfect if you're the kind of person who likes to throw caution to the wind and follow the excitement wherever it leads. However, do bear in mind that most professional pantsers really only pants their first drafts. Once that draft has revealed what the story is really about, they sit down and rewrite everything so it puts events in the right order and all makes sense to the reader. For pantsers, the second draft can look very different to the first.

If you're a more cautious and analytical type, you'll be more inclined to be a plotter and spend a fair amount of time in the beginning creating a well-made structure for your story. The advantage of this is that your first draft will already be fairly well structured, so your second draft probably won't need as much work. A disadvantage is that too much planning can cause you to be over-cautious and you might find yourself stalled as you try to write the perfect first draft. So if you're a plotter, know that no matter how much planning you do, your inspiration and creativity will probably take you off course a bit, and you need to let this happen and do some pantsing as you explore what wants to come through. You might surprise yourself with an even more powerful story.

And if you're by nature a pantser, at some stage you're going to find that a little planning and structuring is your best friend as you try to tame a story that's running out of control or which has inexplicably stopped dead.

In the end, you need a balance of freewheeling inspiration and more coolheaded plotting and planning if you want to write publishable fiction.

Structured vs unstructured stories

Before we get into the nitty-gritty of structure, a few words about the exceptions – the stories with no apparent structure. When it comes to structure, we can broadly divide stories into two tribes – the well-made story and the slice-of-life story.

The well-made story

These stories follow traditional story structure mechanics and principles. They have definite beginnings, middles and ends with all events following logically and progressively to the final climax and resolution. This structure makes these stories easy to read and it's no surprise that most popular literature and genre fiction consist of well-made (or fairly well-made) stories. The American writer Edgar Allan Poe (1809–1849) is credited with defining the form of the well-made short story. It's this kind of story we'll be focusing on in this chapter.

The slice-of-life story

Russian writer Anton Chekhov (1860–1904) had an entirely different take on what a story could be. He sought to write stories that were more like real life – messy and apparently random. His vision of the short story was that of a succession of little scenes composed like a mosaic with little apparent plot or cohesive story. What holds these stories together is the epiphany or emotional payoff at the end. If you want to try a Chekhov story, just Google his story 'Gusev'.

The slice-of-life story, being fairly difficult to pull off successfully, is usually the domain of the more virtuoso and literary writer. For modern slice-of-life stories, try stories published in highbrow magazines like *The New Yorker* and anything by Haruki Murakami (his collections *After the Quake* and *Blind Willow, Sleeping Woman*). You'd be hard-pressed to find a plot with neat beginning, middle and end in most of these stories, and I'm sure Murakami didn't set out with any in mind. He probably just 'pantsed' his way through them and was as surprised as anybody at how they turned out. Which just goes to show you can pants all you want if you know what you're doing and have an innate sense of storytelling.

For most of us, however, a pure pantsing approach isn't going to get us very far and so we should play around with structure first. And there's nothing at all non-literary about structure. You can write a literary masterpiece using the well-made form just as well as the slice-of-life form. But here's a tip – if you want stories to be sellable and make you any kind of income, put your money on the well-made horse. Be literary in your powers of description and your insights about life rather than in your experimentation with literary form (at least until you have a sizable audience who will follow your wild experiments).

Basic story structure

The well-made story has a simple logical structure of three parts – the beginning, the middle and the end. Sounds absurdly simple, but it's what goes into those three parts that makes the story engine work.

The beginning

The beginning is usually referred to by its more writerly term – the *exposition*. We've used that word a lot in this course already so you can probably guess that the beginning is about explaining or giving information of some kind. The exposition of a story usually sets the scene and describes the main character, the situation they're in and the problem they face:

- A character,
- in a situation,
- has a problem.

If this is ringing bells of recognition you'll be right – it's essentially the story premise that we dealt with earlier. You might also remember that the premise is built on some kind of conflict, so the exposition establishes the character, situation and basic conflict they face. The conflict gives rise to a desire to put the situation right and carries with it the stakes for failing to set things right.

The exposition is usually fairly short – probably no more than the first 25% of a full-length work like novel or screenplay, or even shorter in a short story. Full-length stories can stretch the exposition by getting the hero to repeatedly refuse to take action until they're really pushed to take the leap. But that's really a matter for a more advanced plotting workshop. For now, just think of the exposition as the initial outline of the situation and the first encounter with the problem.

Another way to think about the beginning or exposition is that it describes the *ordinary world* that the protagonist finds herself in and an *inciting incident* which disrupts that world and pushes her to the point of action. In a longer work there may be several related inciting incidents which pile on the pressure until she can no longer refuse to act.

The first inciting incident can actually happen before the story opens, so the ordinary world already contains the problem. If that's the case, you'll want one or two more inciting incidents in the exposition to build the tension and compel the hero to act. Once she actually takes action, we cross into the middle section.

Tip: For short stories, your whole exposition with ordinary world and inciting incident will probably be as short as a paragraph or two.

The middle

The middle is what we term the rising action. The exposition told us about the character, their situation and their problem. The middle is all about the character's efforts to solve the problem or endure it as it gets worse and worse:

- The character tries to solve the problem,
- and may fail several times,
- building tension and conflict along the way.

The rising action is generally the longest part of any story, novel or screenplay. It's the beginning and main body of the adventure. It's called 'rising action' because the aim is to increase tension and up the stakes as the story moves along. In a novel or movie, this is when the hero starts the actual adventure and there are many victories, reversals, complications and twists.

In a full-length story, the end of the rising action is often a dark-night-of-the-soul moment when all seems lost and the hero has to reach deep into themselves to find the resources to face the antagonist in one last battle.

All of this is building up to a moment of decisive action – the *climax* – that changes the direction of the story and sets things on the homeward run.

The ending

The end section consists of two sequences – the *climax* and the *resolution*.

The climax

This is the final battle with the antagonist. It may be a physical fight or confrontation or it might just be the moment the protagonist takes some final decisive action that resolves things for either failure or success. The climax is the moment of truth that the hero has been avoiding all along or is slowly building their way towards realising. The climax is a moment of no return. In the rising action, the events were all essentially more of the same, just in different form. Things went well and things went badly, back and forth with growing tension. But with the climax the tension explodes and is released. The hero triumphs or fails decisively. In *Romeo and Juliet*, Romeo drinks the poison and dies. In the movie *Notting Hill*, Hugh Grant's character races to the airport and proposes to the Julia Roberts character.

In a short story, the climax is usually more subtle because there hasn't been a long rising-action sequence to build a huge amount of tension and very high stakes. Instead of dramatic action, the short story usually works towards a moment of surprise, insight, or release of emotion. This is sometimes referred to as the *epiphany*. So if you're writing short stories, you might find it more helpful to think of the climax as an emotional epiphany rather than as some kind of cliff-hanger event.

The resolution

After the dust of the climax has cleared, we are left with the resolution. This is sometimes called the *denouement*. It's where all the loose ends are tied up and we get a glimpse of how the story-world will look now that the storm of the climax has passed. The resolution is usually very short – sometimes only a paragraph. In short stories, the resolution might even be sandwiched in with the climax. Such an ending can be quite abrupt but that can add to the emotional impact and leave the reader in something of a shocked state.

In *Notting Hill*, the resolution is the final scene where Hugh Grant and Julia Roberts are sitting on a park bench in London and it's clear that Julia is pregnant. It's basically a happily-ever-after moment and leaves the viewer with a warm and satisfied glow.

The resolution is the moment of emotional payoff that the reader has been waiting for. In a romance, it's the happy moment after the couple finally declare their love for each other. In a war story, it might be a soldier's realisation that he is not a coward after surviving a major battle. In a domestic drama, it might be the sensation of freedom the protagonist has after she walks out of an abusive marriage.

A different kind of resolution is the 'twist in the tale'. In this kind of ending, the audience is expecting a resolution of one kind but they get something entirely different. For instance, suppose a detective who places a high value on family ties has been tracking a serial killer and finally confronts him in a showdown in a dark room. She gets the bead on him and shoots him dead (the climax). Then she steps forward to pull his mask off to reveal – it's her father! The story ends as a tragedy rather than as the triumph the audience is expecting.

That's the kind of ending that shocks the reader and leaves them with a sense that the story is still continuing. A great tactic, by the way, if you're planning on doing a sequel. The resolution resolves one set of expectations but creates a whole new game that can be played.

To summarise the sequence of the well-made story:

BEGINNING

- A character,
- in a situation (ordinary world),
- has a problem (inciting incidents).

MIDDLE

- The character tries to solve the problem,
- and may fail several times,
- building tension and conflict along the way (rising action),
- until a moment when all seems lost (dark night or pit).

END

- The character makes one final push that succeeds or fails (climax),
- resolving the tension and bringing the story to an end (resolution).

This basic structure of beginning (exposition), middle (rising action) and end (climax & resolution) works for short stories as well as for full-length novels and screenplays. In the longer narratives it becomes the classic three-act plot structure you will almost certainly hear about if you delve deeper into the art of plotting. The beginning is Act 1, the middle is Act 2, and the end is Act 3.

Let's see how this basic structure works for a short story.

Jack and the Beanstalk: An adventure in story structure

Remember the classic fairytale *Jack and the Beanstalk*? Well, turns out it it's the perfect illustration for our discussion on story structure. Take a look and see where I've indicated the basic structure elements.

Jack and the Beanstalk

BEGINNING (EXPOSITION)

Once upon a time, there was a poor widow who lived with her son, Jack, in a cottage at the edge of the village. Their only money came from selling the milk of their old cow, Bessy. But one sad day, Bessy gave no milk, so they had no money at all.

"Oh, what shall we do?" cried the widow. "We're going to die of hunger."

"I know," said Jack. "We'll have to sell Bessy. Then we can buy some seed and plant some vegetables to sell. And get some chickens to lay eggs."

"Good idea," said the widow. "Go to market tomorrow and sell Old Bessy."

MIDDLE (RISING ACTION)

So the next morning Jack led Bessy by the halter and headed off to market. He hadn't gone far when he met a strange-looking old man. "Good morning, Jack," said the man.

"Good morning to you," said Jack, wondering how the man knew his name.

"Where are you off to this fine morning?" asked the man.

"I'm going to market to sell our cow, Bessy."

"Oh, that's so sad you have to sell your only cow," said the man, looking concerned. "But for good people in circumstances such as yours, I have a special deal." The little, old man looked around to make sure no one was watching and then opened his hand to show Jack what he held.

"Beans?" asked Jack, looking a little confused.

"Three magical beans to be exact. If you plant them, by the next morning they'll have grown right up to the sky," promised the little man. "They're worth a fortune, but I'm prepared to trade them for that scrawny old cow of yours."

"Are you quite sure they're magical?" asked Jack. "If they're not I'll get into such trouble."

"Oh yes, I'm certain indeed. Tell you what ... if it doesn't turn out to be true, you can have your cow back."

"All right," said Jack, as he handed over Bessy's halter, pocketed the beans and headed back home to show his mother.

"That was quick," said his mother. "How much did you get for Old Bess?"

Jack reached into his pocket and brought out the beans. "I got these magical beans, mother. They're worth a fortune. You just plant them and then ..."

"What!" cried Jack's mother. "Magical beans? Now you've surely ruined us." And with that she burst into tears.

Jack ran upstairs to his little room and threw the beans angrily out the window. How could I have been so foolish, he thought. I've broken my mother's heart. I'm a bad son indeed. Jack went to bed and after much tossing and turning eventually dropped into a troubled sleep.

When Jack woke up the next morning, his room looked strange. The sun was shining into part of it like it normally did, and yet all the rest was quite dark. So Jack jumped up and dressed himself and went to the window. And there he gasped with amazement for the beans he had thrown out of the window into the garden had sprung up into a huge beanstalk which went up and up into the sky.

Being a curious and adventurous fellow, Jack got up onto the windowsill and then jumped straight onto the beanstalk. He began climbing up, using the leaves and twisty vines like the rungs of a ladder. At least he got so high he disappeared into a cloud. He climbed some more and when he came out of the top of the cloud he stood blinking in amazement at what he saw, for there were fields and little houses and a long, winding road leading off into the distance. Jack jumped off the beanstalk onto the road and began walking. After a short while he saw that the road led to a castle. Oh good, thought Jack, I'm getting awfully hungry. Maybe they'll have some tea and cake for me.

Jack ran up the road toward the castle and just as he reached it, the door swung open to reveal a horrible lady giant with big, glaring eyes. As soon as Jack saw her he turned to run away, but she caught him, and dragged him into the castle. "Don't be in such a hurry," she said in a booming voice. "I'm sure a growing boy like you would like a nice cup of tea and a big breakfast."

The giant lady took him inside and sat him down at a huge table that was as high as his head. Then she put a pot of water on the fire and began cutting some cheese and bread. "Here," she said, giving Jack a huge plate, "I hope I haven't made too much." Jack said thank you and took a bite of bread. It was very fresh and tasty. He was just about to take a second bite when thump! thump! thump! the whole house began to tremble with the noise of giant footsteps.

"Oh dear! It's my husband," said the giant woman, wringing her hands. "There's nothing he likes better than boys on toast and I haven't any bread left. Come quick and jump in here." And she hurried Jack into a large copper pot sitting beside the stove just as her husband, the giant, came in.

He ducked inside the kitchen and said, "I'm ready for my breakfast – I'm so hungry I could eat three cows. "Ah, what's this I smell?" He sniffed the air again and then began roaring a terrible rhyme:

Fee-fi-fo-fum,
I smell the blood of an Englishman,
Be he alive, or be he dead
I'll grind his bones to make my bread.

"Nonsense, dear," said his wife, "we haven't had a boy for breakfast in years. Now you go and wash up and by the time you come back your breakfast will be ready for you."

So the giant went off to tidy up. Jack was about to make a run for it when the woman stopped him. "Wait until he's asleep," she said, "he always has a little snooze after breakfast."

Jack peeked out of the copper pot just as the giant returned to the kitchen carrying a basket with a sickly looking, white hen. The giant poked the hen and growled, "Lay", and the hen laid an egg made of gold. The giant took the egg and put it in a chest filled with golden eggs.

After his breakfast, the giant went to the closet and pulled out a golden harp with the face of a sad girl. He prodded the harp and growled, "Play", and the harp began to play a gentle tune. Then the giant began to nod his head and to snore until the house shook.

When he was quite sure the giant was asleep, Jack crept out of the copper pot and began to tiptoe out of the kitchen. Just as he was about to leave, he heard the sound of the harp-girl weeping. Jack sighed and returned to the kitchen. He grabbed the sickly hen and the singing harp and began to tiptoe back out. But this time the hen gave a cackle which woke the giant, and just as Jack got out of the house he heard him calling, "Wife, wife, what have you done with my white hen and my golden harp?"

END (CLIMAX)

Jack ran as fast as he could and the giant came stomping after him down the winding road. When he got to the beanstalk the giant was only twenty yards away. He jumped onto the beanstalk and began clambering down through the cloud as fast as he could. When he looked up through the cloud he saw the giant's angry face yelling at him:

Fee-fi-fo-fum,
I smell the blood of an Englishman,
Be he alive, or be he dead
I'll grind his bones to make my bread.

The giant swung himself down onto the beanstalk which shook with his weight. Jack slipped and slid down the beanstalk as quickly as he could, followed by the giant.

As he neared the bottom, Jack called out, "Mother! Hurry, bring me an axe." And his mother came rushing out with an axe in her hand. The moment Jack got to the ground he took the axe and began chopping at the beanstalk. Before long the beanstalk began to shake and shiver and the giant hung onto the beanstalk for dear life. But then Jack gave one last big chop with the axe, and the beanstalk came crashing to the ground, bringing the giant with it. And that was the end of him.

END (RESOLUTION)

The singing harp thanked Jack for rescuing her from the giant – she had hated being locked up in the closet and wanted nothing more than to sit in the farmhouse window and sing for everyone who walked by.

Jack and his mother took care of the white hen and nursed her back to health. When she was nice and plump again, she began to lay a golden egg every day. Jack used the money from selling the golden eggs to buy back Old Bess and to fix up the cottage. And every week they invited all the poor people in the village for a lovely big meal, complete with music from the singing harp.

And so Jack, his mother, Old Bess, the golden harp and the white hen lived happily ever after.

Analysing the story

The exposition

The exposition is the starting situation and introduction to the characters. So in this story it's the short section where Jack and his mother are introduced and their core problem – lack of money – is stated. It ends at the moment Jack leaves home and goes to the market.

This story provides a great illustration of the exposition because it's very often a 'leaving home' moment that signals the transition to the narrative. In this case, Jack literally leaves home, signalling the start of an adventure. In other stories this can be more figurative, such as the arrival of an unexpected guest who disrupts the status quo and starts a series of conflicts. The 'home' that is left is the original situation, also known in plot-speak as the ordinary world.

The rising action

This is the main body of the story. So it's everything from the moment Jack sets out with Old Bess until just before his final battle with the giant

The climax

The climax is the final, decisive confrontation with the antagonist. In this case, it's the passage or mini-scene that builds up to and includes Jack chopping down the beanstalk. The moment of chopping down the beanstalk is the actual climax, with the preceding lines the setup to this moment.

The resolution

The resolution ties up loose ends and gives a glimpse of the new world that comes into being with the defeat of the antagonist (or triumph of the antagonist if things go badly for the hero). In this case, the antagonist is soundly defeated, leading to Jack and his mother becoming rich and resolving the core conflict of their poverty.

Mixing things up in the modern story

I chose *Jack and the Beanstalk* because it illustrates the phases of the structure quite clearly. However, not all well-made stories are this clearly delineated. In fact, the modern trend is to start stories quite dramatically and to jump straight into the action or into a piece of dialogue with little or no explanation about the situation or characters.

This means that the exposition section is not always written with typical expository text (text that explains things explicitly) but tends to go straight into narrative-style text. Don't get confused here – the term 'exposition' covers two things: exposition text as a mode of writing and exposition as the beginning section or first act in a three-act plot structure. Technically, the exposition section is everything from the start of the story to the point where the protagonist takes an action that commits them to the adventure. The more contemporary writing style keeps the exposition section but drops some of the traditional explanatory text in favour of narrative text.

Exposition is then scattered organically into the narrative so that the reader picks up on any necessary background as the story develops. The advantage of doing it this way is that you can get a stronger opening and create more suspense by leaving the reader guessing about the context.

For example, suppose you want to give the reader the information that Jack and his mother live on a farm. Here's how you might do it as exposition and as narrative:

Exposition: Jack and his mother lived on a farm.

Narrative: "Jack, take your shoes off before coming into the house. Now there's mud and cow poop everywhere!" "Sorry, mum," said Jack, breathlessly.

The first example is classic exposition – a *telling* of necessary information. The second example gives the reader all the essential information without stating it obviously. We've essentially replaced exposition with narrative and created a more lively passage. Now it's up to you to decide whether this suits the style and voice of your story.

If this advice to scatter exposition into narrative is sounding familiar to you it's because we worked with it in the chapter on description. I gave a recommendation that where possible, you should describe things 'in motion' (as they unfold organically) rather than by dropping in discrete chunks of exposition. So that's all we're doing here – cutting out lengthy explanations in the opening section and working the information into the story as it unfolds. And once again, this is not an absolute rule but rather a consideration that you can try out and see if it improves your story.

Story structure for memoir and creative non-fiction

Structure for memoir can follow a very similar pattern. In Chapter 4, I outlined a typical memoir premise as the following:

- A character: You or someone else you're writing about.
- A situation: The subject of your memoir. For instance, your year spent living as a writer in Paris or your experiences covering the war in Iraq.
- A lesson: What did you learn from this experience or how did your life change as a result of it? Instead of a lesson you could have a theme and arrange your narration to explore that theme in detail.

Here's an example premise that states the character, situation and lesson:

> When a young reporter is sent to cover the Allied invasion of Iraq, she discovers that victory is not the end of war but merely the first step on a journey into darkness.

As you can see, this is very close to the fiction structure we've just been discussing, which begins with a character in a situation with a problem. In a memoir, the way you get to your final insight will often follow many of the milestones or plot points of fiction. For instance, there'll be some kind of exposition and then you'll get going with the body of the story and you might even have a dark moment that leads to your final insight. The same goes for any creative non-fiction that describes the life of someone else or the development of an idea. You'll generally begin with an exposition, then move into the body of the story, then present some kind of surprising conclusion that shocks or satisfies the reader.

Do bear in mind, however, that memoir and non-fiction have other possible story structures, so don't try too hard to squeeze your story into the structure I've been discussing. You might find that you can use elements of the fiction formula in your non-fiction to create a more engaging and dynamic text. As always, experiment with different forms and find what works best for you and your particular story.

Next steps in plotting

This chapter has presented a fairly basic introduction to the subject of plotting and will be enough to get you started. In fact, it will put you well ahead of all those writers who are working away without any knowledge of story structure at all. However, we haven't really had the space to go into the subject in enough detail to see exactly how to weave the inner and outer journeys of your protagonists together. We also haven't looked at all the beats or key moments in a full plot outline. So, if you are writing a long work such as a novel or screenplay, I recommend you study the subject further as it can save you much rewriting and frustration. You will find helpful books on the subject at your local bookstore or on Amazon.

Context of this lesson

Knowing about basic story structure is critical for your journey as an author because:
- If your story doesn't have a premise and some kind of plot structure that keeps the story on track, it's just not

going to sell – either through mainstream publishing or through self-publishing. And yes, this includes most literary fiction too.

- Agents and publishers are going to ask you to summarise the plot for them before they even look at your manuscript. You'll need an intriguing premise and a tightly scripted plot outline that promises a satisfying climax and resolution. And if you are aiming to self-publish, your readers and critics are going to demand the same information.
- Knowing about story structure helps you generate new content when you run out of ideas (more on that in the next chapter).

Summary

The main ideas from this chapter:
- Structurally, there are two basic types of stories – the well-made story and the slice-of-life story.
- The well-made story has a simple logical structure of three parts – the beginning (exposition), the middle (rising action), and the end (climax and resolution).
- In modern stories, the trend is to jump straight into the action or dialogue. Any necessary background information is then scattered organically into the narrative.
- Memoir can follow a similar structure of exposition, rising action, moment of crisis or insight, and final resolution. Other structures are also common.

Exercises

Placing a scene in a story structure

Look at the scenes you've already written. Choose at least one and imagine that it forms part of a complete story. Then consider which part of the story structure it fits into. Is it part of the exposition, the rising action, the climax or the resolution?

For example, let's take one of the scene fragments I wrote in the chapter on Description:

> Father Anselm and Gregory trudged up the hill path, taking care not to slip on the treacherous shards of wet rock that slithered down from the slopes above them. Gregory stood to catch his breath and looked up at the castle. It loomed over them – grey, forbidding and absolutely silent but for the sighing of wind through its turrets and spires. "Come on," said Father Anselm, leaning on his staff. "There'll be a fire in the great hall. And warm food."
>
> Gregory said nothing but pulled his cloak tighter around him as an icy gust blew down from distant Mount Arack. The snow-capped peaks of the mountain lay in a shifting, watery light that brought no warmth but spoke only of a dark yet to come.

As I look at it now, this scene seems most likely to be part of the rising action. The two characters have obviously been on a journey and they're looking for something. Perhaps this castle is where they will do battle with the antagonist. On the other hand, it could be part of an exposition sequence and the story will only really begin once they enter the castle and weird things start happening.

Now over to you. Do this exercise for at least one of your sketches. This is a warm-up for the next lesson where you'll see how to take your chosen scene and map out the other scenes needed to build a complete story.

CHAPTER 13

Running the Story Generator

In the previous chapter you were introduced to basic story structure and you got a feel for how stories unfold from beginning to end. Now you're going to put this knowledge to work and see how structure actually generates story.

You see, the real magic of story structure is that it is co-creative – it suggests what you need to write next when you run out of ideas and sit there twiddling your pen wondering how on earth you're going to stretch your few meagre pages into a full-length story. However, you really don't have to start out knowing everything about how the story is going to work out or even how it's going to end – all you need is a glimmer of an idea and a basic knowledge of structure. Then you get your Story Generator fired up.

The Story Generator in action

The Story Generator is very simple. It has two ingredients – a seed idea or scene and a story structure template. By this stage in the course, you should already have quite a few story ideas and scenes and you have a basic idea of story structure. So you're all set.

Step 1

Take an A4 piece of paper or open a Word document and create headings for the main points of your foundation and story structure. You'll have the following headings:

Premise:

Exposition:

Rising action:

Climax:

Resolution:

Under each main heading you can also put subheadings for scenes that you know you'll need. For instance, I know that all exposition sections will need an opening scene and an inciting incident scene. Quite often, the opening scene *is* the inciting incident and you don't have to mention them separately. But if not, be sure to include details of both your opening scene and the scene in which the main disturbance appears. You might also need to give some backstory, so you could list this under its own subheading.

Step 2

Take your existing premise or scenes that you've sketched out and place them into the structure. Just write the premise or a one-line summary of each scene and file it under Premise, Exposition, Rising action, Climax or Resolution. Note that in short stories it's not always easy to think in terms of discrete scenes for each plot point – it's sometimes more like scene parts or sometimes just individual sentences or paragraphs. Either way, write down your indication of what needs to happen under each section of your plot structure.

Step 3

Now look at your structure and see where content is missing. Then write brief descriptions of scenes that need to be added to make everything fit together. For instance, if you've written a single scene that seems to be the ending of a story, work backwards from there to fill in what needs to happen to get the protagonists to that point.

Important: If some of your existing scenes don't fit into the structure – don't put them in. This is the point where the story structure will tell you what it needs. If a scene doesn't advance the plot, deepen character, fill in backstory or perform some other necessary function, leave it out (at least for now).

Also note that with this structure outline you don't need to list every scene if you're writing a long work – just note the most important things that need to happen. And if you're writing a short story, some of the different parts of the structure might be covered in a single scene. The only important thing now is just to write down the main turning points in the story, whether those will take several scenes to unfold or just a paragraph.

Story Generator example

I'll show you two ways to use the Story Generator – one where we start with a scene or two from somewhere in the story, and the other where we start with only a premise. In the first example below, I'll start with a single scene and then generate a whole story.

1. Beginning with a scene

As my seed idea I'm going to use the sketch for the murder mystery I gave in the chapter on Scenes. You can read it again here to refresh your memory.

Scene title: Finding the body

First they tied him to a tree with his arms stretched back around the trunk and the wrists bound with cable ties. Then they went to work on him. Something like a cheese grater or a wood rasp, judging from the ragged strips of ripped flesh on his face and chest. I took a step back from the corpse and held the back of my hand to my nose. Early morning mist hung in the dreary woodland, the scent of wet earth and leaves struck through with the odour of rot. A constable cordoned off the area with yellow and blue tape while a forensics officer zipped himself into a sterile bodysuit.

I heard a sound behind me and turned and saw a grey-haired man walking up from the dirt path, pulling on rubber gloves as he walked. DCI Penny, I assumed. He stopped next to me and peered at the body and grimaced. Then he looked at me. "And who are you?" he said.

"DS Sherwood," I said. "Transferred from Birmingham yesterday."

"It just follows you wherever you go, doesn't it?"

"Sir?"

"The stench of death. Of evil. You think you're leaving the city for a quiet life in the country but it finds you anyway."

"I wasn't ... well, I mean, I came because of the wife, see. She doesn't do well in the city. And my boy. He ran into some bad company back home. I mean, back there."

The chief inspector turned from me abruptly and took a step closer to the corpse. "What do you see, DS Sherwood?" he said, leaning over the body, unaffected by the cloying smell.

"Torture, Sir."

"And what more?"

"Well, I'd say it's a message of some kind. Bit too elaborate for the benefit of its recipient alone, if you know what I mean."

DCI Penny looked at the corpse grimly and nodded. "That looks about right," he said. Then he stood back, gave me a steely eyed nod, and walked back to the woodland track and without another word.

He'd guessed right about me leaving the city for a quiet life in the country. That had been the plan anyway. Just routine burglaries and vandalism, they'd said.

Nothing more than the usual antisocial behaviour and some rowdiness around the pubs on a Friday night. But as I stood looking at that corpse I knew the promise had been a lie. Death and trouble had followed me. I wouldn't tell Emily. Not just yet anyway.

When I wrote this scene, I didn't have any idea of its context and had no plans for taking it further. I just wanted a scene that I could use for demonstration purposes in this course. So now I'm curious about whether there's actually a story lurking somewhere in it.

In the first step I'll just write out a blank story structure template. Then I'll take my existing scene and plug it into the structure. I'll also add any other explanatory notes that occur to me. This is how it looks for the story I'm building:

Story Generator Template

PREMISE: __

EXPOSITION:

–Opening scene: *Finding the body*. DS Sherwood finds the first victim and meets DCI Penny (scene already written).

–Inciting incident: As above (opening scene is the inciting incident).

–Backstory: He's been transferred and is looking for a quiet life. He's a brilliant detective but is sick of dealing with evil. He wants out. (Partly covered in the opening scene. Weave more backstory detail into upcoming scenes in the Exposition.)

RISING ACTION: __

CLIMAX: __
RESOLUTION: __

At this stage, this is all I know about my story. I don't know how it ends or even if it's worth telling. So now I'll fill in more of the template and see if it takes me anywhere interesting:

PREMISE: __

EXPOSITION:

–Opening scene: *Finding the body.* DS Sherwood finds the first victim and meets DCI Penny (scene already written).

–Inciting incident: As above (opening scene is the inciting incident).

–Backstory: He's been transferred and is looking for a quiet life. He's a brilliant detective but is sick of dealing with evil. He wants out. (Partly covered in the opening scene. Weave more backstory detail into upcoming scenes in the Exposition.)

RISING ACTION: Sherwood has to look for the killer. The trail takes him back to Birmingham and three similar murders that took place while he was still working there.

He discovers that the murderer seems to be following him – all the murders are linked to him and where he works. He eventually identifies the killer – a man he put in prison years ago and who has recently been released. But ...

CLIMAX: ... he realises the killer is actually out to get revenge on him, so he races home. Too late – the killer kidnaps his son. A chase ensues. Sherwood shoots the killer. Then finds that his son is already dead.

RESOLUTION: It's five years later. He is now a senior police officer, but his wife has left him. His desire to live peacefully and have nothing to do with evil in society has not been fulfilled. He visits the grave of his son and remembers the conversation from the opening scene:

"It just follows you wherever you go, doesn't it?"

"Sir?"

"The stench of death. Of evil. You think you're leaving the city for a quiet life in the country, but it finds you anyway."

The underlying story theme is revealed: Sometimes, the bad guys win (but you have to keep playing anyway).

I just made all of that up right now for the purpose of this exercise – and I think it actually works! It's very rough and sketchy, but it already has the shape of a full-length story that might actually be worth writing. If I hadn't gone through the Story Generator exercise, I wouldn't have come up with all that content and the surprise ending. I really had no clue it would end up being a tragedy rather than a triumph. The story just generated itself that way. And by writing it out like this I discovered the theme of the story – *Sometimes, the bad guys win, but you have to keep playing anyway.* We haven't covered theme in this course as it's a bit advanced, but now that it has showed up spontaneously I can include it in the plan (perhaps as a heading called 'Theme' under 'Premise'). It's worth pausing a moment to take in the significance of this – the theme only revealed itself *after* I did the work on story structure. This illustrates my point that the formal structure helps you generate content – it reveals the hidden story beneath the bolts of inspiration and the scattered scenes that don't seem to add up to anything like a full story. As a writer, you really can start to trust that your inner mind has a plan for your story, even if you don't consciously know what it is at first. When you take the time to lay out the story framework, the hidden order is revealed.

2. Beginning from a premise or story idea

Suppose you haven't written any scenes yet and all you've got is your premise or a basic story idea. That's the perfect time to crank up the Story Generator. Just write your premise/idea at the top of the page and then work out which scenes you'll need in order to dramatise it. Remember that the premise usually describes the Exposition and maybe a hint of the rising action or climax. So you've got some pointers for your first scenes already.

In this example, I'll use the same DS Sherwood murder mystery idea and I'll start by writing down the premise. Then I'll fill in the scenes that are needed in order for the premise to be fulfilled. I'll put the elements of the premise in italics so you can see what I'm doing.

Story Generator Template

PREMISE: A detective transfers from a city to a rural village hoping for a quiet life for himself and his family. But when a body is found in the woods on his first day at work, he is drawn into a life and death struggle with a killer seeking revenge at all costs.

EXPOSITION:

–Opening scene: (*But when a body is found in the woods on his first day at work...*) Opening scene to be written: DS Sherwood finds body in the woods. It looks like a ritual killing. He is put in charge of the investigation.

–Inciting incident: As above (opening scene is the inciting incident).

–Backstory: (*A detective transfers from a city to a rural village hoping for a quiet life for himself and his family.*) Weave this backstory into the opening scenes.

RISING ACTION: Sherwood investigates the killing. His search takes him back to Birmingham where he discovers that the killer is actually seeking revenge on him.

(*... he is drawn into a life-or-death struggle with a killer seeking revenge at all costs*). Sherwood pursues the killer while the killer pursues Sherwood. In the build-up to the climax he realises his family is in danger and races home.

CLIMAX: _____

RESOLUTION: _____

I've still got to fill out the Climax and Resolution, but I won't do that now as it will be the same as my previous example, and you've already seen that.

As a final point, remember that if you don't like the outcome of your first run of the generator you can just retrace your steps to the point where things seem to go off in one direction and make a different choice. Then you can just work through the generator again from that point and see where it takes you.

Now that you've seen the power of the Story Generator at work it's time to turn it loose on your own stories.

Summary

The Story Generator will help you flesh out a complete story from just a premise or a few scenes:
- Begin by writing down headings for all the main plot points of the general story structure: Premise/Story idea, Exposition (Opening scene, Inciting incident, Backstory), Rising action, Climax, Resolution.
- Then fill in the spaces next to each heading with notes about content that you already have.
- Look at the headings with no content and see what still needs to be developed to complete the story. Add brief notes of scenes to be written.

Exercises

By now you should have some interesting story premises and scenes you've been working on, so here's your chance to see how they might fit together.

1. Generate a story

Step 1: From your existing work, select one of the following:
- A single scene or a collection of scenes that seem like they belong in the same story
- A premise on its own
- A premise and a few associated scenes

Step 2: Take your scenes and/or premise and then populate the Story Generator template given below. Make brief notes in the template that indicate where your existing scenes belong.

Step 3: See what's still missing and then fill in the blanks with descriptions or outlines of what needs to happen.

Story Generator Template

PREMISE: __

EXPOSITION (Beginning): __

    Opening scene: __

    Inciting incident: __

    Backstory: __

RISING ACTION (Middle): __

CLIMAX (End): __

RESOLUTION (End): __

2. Write a scene

Write at least one scene suggested by the Story Generator in Exercise 1 above. For instance, if you worked out that your rising action needs your protagonist to have an argument with their spouse, write that scene.

CHAPTER 14

Opening Lines

Here we are in the last lesson of the course and you're now marvellously equipped to bring a short story to completion or to make real progress on a longer work. However, there's one more thing we need to cover to really get you set for success – and that's the matter of first scenes and opening lines.

One of the biggest mistakes made by beginner authors is failing to write a strong opening paragraph. The story usually begins with some background exposition or a random event that doesn't seem to have any clear purpose in the story. The result is a lack of drama and any good reason to continue reading. The fact is that these days you don't have the luxury of beginning a story just anywhere and assuming readers will follow you and pay good money for the privilege of doing so. Readers pick up books in bookstores and scan the first few lines and make their decision within seconds. In this brief slice of time, you have to stun them, seduce them or entertain them in some other fabulous manner so they keep reading. If they make it to the bottom of the page, you've achieved your first victory. If they don't, it's either because they're hurrying to the cashier with your book or they've shelved it and are looking at someone else's opening lines.

Your first paragraph is the most important passage you'll write in your whole book. So don't mess about with background stuff and random scenes going nowhere. Hit them with drama and get them asking the only question that matters: What happens next?

To do this, you've got to make two choices when opening your story:

- Which scene do you start with (the subject matter)?
- How do you open that scene (the words on the page)?

Which scene to start with

You already know from our discussion on story structure that the beginning is generally where we give some exposition on the character, their situation and their problem or conflict. The moment you introduce conflict, you evoke questions in the mind of the reader, and this compels them to read more to find out how the conflict is resolved.

Conflict begins when something happens that disrupts the protagonist's ordinary world and compels them to take action to resolve the problem. In a short story, you will jump straight into the main conflict. But in a full-length story you might want to begin with a precursor to the main conflict. For instance, in *Star Wars Episode IV* (the very first Star Wars that was made), the film opens with a brief prelude and then properly begins when we see Luke Skywalker repairing a droid which suddenly beams a holographic image of a Princess Leia making an appeal for help from someone called Obi-Wan. This enigmatic statement is enough to set up questions that the audience wants answered. Who is she, who is Obi-Wan, and what kind of trouble is she in?

We're still some way from meeting the antagonist, Darth Vader, and the start of the main conflict, but this scene is the harbinger of the conflict that will soon engulf Luke. We've got a character, in a situation, with a disruption. At first it's not a serious disruption – merely a question. But it's compelling enough to make us want to find out more. When Luke follows the thread of those questions, he soon enough finds himself in trouble he could never have imagined.

The lesson for us is to start with a disrupting event that gives rise to questions in the mind of the reader or viewer. In writer-speak, this setup is known as the *hook*. It hooks readers and stops them from getting away. Your first paragraphs have one purpose only: to hook the reader. And they do this by setting up conflict that creates questions that evoke the reader's curiosity.

I've sketched an idea for an opening scene below, so let's see if it will work:

> Joe, newly married, walks home from work feeling happy. He stops and buys a bunch of flowers for his wife. Just then there's the sound of hooting and people are shouting in the streets. He goes outside, clutching the flowers, to find that war has been declared.

In this scene, Joe's ordinary world is briefly described (he's newly married and happy), and then the disruption comes (war is declared). This leads to questions for the reader about what will happen next. So this should work quite well as an opening scene, as long as it's written in an engaging style that brings out the contrast between his happiness and the approach of war.

Which brings us to the second set of choices you have to make about your opening lines – how to write them.

Which lines to open with

You've chosen your opening scene and made sure it's got a hook that will spark the curiosity of your reader. Now let's zoom in even closer and look at the very first sentences of that scene. And guess what – that's got to be a hook too. A one-paragraph hook. Preferably even a one-line hook!

So how do you do that?

You arouse curiosity. Simple as that. And luckily for us there are some tried and trusted ways of doing so:

1. Start with a disruption – something happens that creates immediate questions in the reader's mind.
2. Start with a setting description that creates a sense of movement and seduces with its delicious words, inviting the reader to step into another world.
3. Start right in the middle of the action (*in medias res*).
4. Start with dialogue.
5. Start with a startling, resonant statement that shocks the reader into paying attention.

I'll give some examples of each one below. Notice how each one has been crafted to catch your attention in some way.

1. Start with a disruption – something happens

With this kind of beginning, you don't waste any time with explanations about who characters are or how they got there – you jump straight in with a disturbance that sets the story going. Typical disturbances might be a phone call in the middle of the night, a car breaking down in the desert, an accident, the arrival of an unexpected guest or the unexpected departure of a loved one.

> As soon as she finished dressing, Laura went to the front door, just in time to see the LA Police Department squad car pull to the curb in front of the house. —Dean Koontz, *The Door to December*.

> It was a wrong number that started it, the telephone ringing three times in the dead of night, and the voice on the other end asking for someone he was not. —Paul Auster, *City of Glass*

2. Start with a resonant, scene-setting description

This is a great way to begin if you are a word-artist and you want to appeal directly to readers who appreciate writing style and texture. It's got to be artfully written and create a mood. But it's also got to have movement. For instance, if you open with a paragraph describing the stark landscape of Monument Valley in Utah, make sure that the second paragraph zooms in until we can see the bad man in a black hat riding slowly towards the town. The landscape description will set the mood and tell us something about the character we're about to meet. For this type of intro to work you need poetry and movement.

> The Santa Ana blew hot from the desert, shrivelling the last of the spring grass into whiskers of pale straw. Only the oleanders thrived, their delicate poisonous blooms, their dagger green leaves. —Janet Fitch, *White Oleander*

These opening lines from *White Oleander* are full of the sense of foreboding – something bad is going to happen. And it's going to happen in resonant and luscious prose.

> There was a desert wind blowing that night. It was one of those hot dry Santa Anas that come down through the mountain passes and curl your hair and make your nerves jump and your skin itch. On nights like that every booze party ends in a fight. Meek little wives feel the edge of the carving knife and study their husbands' necks. Anything can happen. —Raymond Chandler, *Red Wind*

The image of those meek wives with carving knives is an arresting statement of contrast and conflict that is impossible to ignore. There's clearly something about this Santa Ana that brings out the weird in people. In both these examples, a feature of nature sets a scene of tension and approaching violence.

3. Start with action (in medias res)

Open in the midst of some action with no explanation about the cause of the action. Allow the reader to figure out the situation for themselves as they continue reading.

> I clasp the flask between my hands even though the warmth from the tea has long since leached into the frozen air. —Suzanne Collins, *Catching Fire*

4. Start with dialogue

Jump straight into a crucial piece of dialogue laced with conflict and disruption. This is a form of beginning *in medias res*.

"What are you going to do when you leave school?" asked Alexander.

"I'm hoping to join the KGB," Vladimir replied. — Jeffrey Archer, *Heads You Win*

*

"You are full of nightmares," Harriet tells me. —James Baldwin, *This Morning, This Evening, So Soon*

Note: Use this kind of opening with caution. It can be a bit too much of a leap for the reader if the first thing they encounter is lots of dialogue and they don't know who is speaking. Make sure you clue the reader in as soon as you can because if they feel lost for too long they'll jump ship. Use your judgement and intuition here.

5. Start with a powerful, surprising statement

A brilliant way to start is to make a short, resonant statement about a situation. By resonant, I mean something that has the power to move the reader and elicit some kind of reaction from them. Read the examples of first lines from novels below and see how they use surprise, contrast, boldness, controversy – anything that causes the reader to pay attention and get intrigued. The lines should be so resonant they become quotable.

It is a truth, universally acknowledged, that a single man in possession of a good fortune, must be in want of a wife. —Jane Austen, *Pride and Prejudice*

*

All happy families are alike; each unhappy family is unhappy in its own way. —Leo Tolstoy, *Anna Karenina*

*

It was a queer, sultry summer, the summer they electro-cuted the Rosenbergs, and I didn't know what I was doing in New York. —Sylvia Plath, *The Bell Jar*

*

We are on our way to Budapest. Bastard and Chipo and Godknows and Sbho and Stina and me. We are going even though we are not allowed to cross Mzilikazi Road, even though Bastard is supposed to be watching his sis-ter Fraction, even though Mother would kill me dead if she found out; we are just going. —NoViolet Bulawayo, *We All Need New Names*

*

They shoot the white girl first. —Toni Morrison, *Paradise*

Just read that first line from *Paradise* again: 'They shoot the white girl first'. That's what I mean by short, resonant and quotable. It's a declaration of the author's authority, a bold statement of their control of the story and its presentation. So aim for these bold, poetic, resonant lines that immediately sig-nal to the reader that you're not messing about – the story begins here, now, and it's time to get on board.

Tip: Create immediacy in your opening lines by adding con-crete details. Use a person's name – don't just call them 'the man' or 'the girl' unless you purposely want to keep their identi-ty cloaked. Use the names of plants, animals, streets, buildings and aspects of the landscape (e.g., Santa Ana wind, oleanders, the Rosenbergs, Mzilikazi Road, Chipho, Godknows).

Opening lines in memoir and creative non-fiction

All the principles I've outlined above work just as well for memoir and creative non-fiction.

> The lawyer Jan Schlichtmann was awakened by the telephone at eight-thirty on a Saturday morning in mid-July. —Jonathan Harr, *A Civil Action*.

The example above is a non-fiction work, but see how it jumps in with a named character and a specific disturbance. We want to know what the phone call is about – we're hooked.

I've written an example opening scene for a memoir to see if we can improve it:

> I was born in 1932 in London and went to school in Camberwell. I don't remember the name of the school; it's hardly important now. In fact, I remember little of those first years because everything was wonderfully ordinary. Then the war came and father went off to the army and Mum and I moved in with Aunt Meg whose husband was also off to war. I had imagined the war would have something to do about not going to school anymore, but in this I was to be disappointed. School continued as usual except on air-raid days or when we had to queue with our food stamps to get rations for the week. It was difficult for us but there was still time to play and a bombed-out building was the perfect place to run around being soldiers with the other boys of the neighbourhood. It never really felt real – the bombs al-

ways hit other people's houses and I always assumed we were exempt from the general destruction going on around us. The terrible thing that happened to others would never happen to us. That's what I thought, at least, until a particular morning in March, 1941, when everything changed.

So be honest here – did that grab you?

I'm guessing it probably didn't. The passage opens with expository text that sketches the character and background using a chronological arrangement, starting at birth. The hook only comes at the end with the statement 'when everything changed'. It's really a chronicle of events rather than a story.

Now I'll try reworking it to put the hook where it belongs – right at the start.

My world ended at 5:30 on a Tuesday morning in March, 1941. I know the time precisely because it was always the time Mum would come upstairs to my room and wake me so I could get ready for school. On that morning she came into my room and shook me by the shoulder and as I rose upward from sleep and saw her smile there came a sharp, whistling howl from above and then a flash of unearthly light erased the room and flung me backwards into darkness. They found her later amidst the rubble. Parts of her. This is what they told me in the hospital when I was able to speak. I don't remember crying. The next day they put me on a train with a hundred other children headed out for the country where the bombs didn't fall. Strange how it's the small things one remembers after 70 years. Her smile, the cold of a winter's morning, and that godawful shriek from the heavens that tore my world apart.

What do you think about this version?

The first line now has a hook – the question of how the author's world ended – and it opens with a dramatic moment rather than a date of birth. So I think it's a better beginning, though you might have ideas for something even better. The main point here is that even though you're writing about fact rather than fiction, the way you *arrange and tell* the events will use the principles of fiction and narrative.

Opening line clunkers

We've had a look at examples of how to write great opening lines with powerful hooks. So let's spend a moment contemplating the mistakes that will sink your book at page 1.

'Guy alone in his room, thinking'

Rule number 1 – never start with a long passage of thought. This is a favourite of writers who haven't really got a powerful story and think it's enough to amaze readers with their angsty musings about nothing in particular. Unless those thoughts are truly poetic or bizarre and build up to some kind of conflict within a matter of seconds, you haven't got a story at all – just a collection of scenes. Nobody wants your thoughts about life. They want real people making difficult choices and facing challenges. Your characters can share some thoughts, but let those be relevant to the moment and part of the unfolding action. And yes, this applies to you literary writers too! Let your literariness come through in the depth of your characters, the gritty realism of your storytelling and your finely wrought prose.

Ask yourself if you've written a hook or just some text that you think has amazing ideas in it. If it's a hook, keep it. If not, chuck it.

'Dudes drinking beer and shooting pool'

This mistake is about starting with random scenes that you think are totally cool but don't advance the story at all. And yes, it's not just about dudes in bars. It's conversations that go nowhere. It's meetings with friends and talking about the weather. If you're doing it on purpose to set people up for some kind of conflict then yes, it might work, but the key here is *on purpose*. You've got to write it in a way that makes the reader feel some weird shit is gonna go down any moment now. This is foreshadowing. It's a legitimate way to create a hook because it promises movement and drama. Still, I'd shy away from this as a beginner writer. This kind of opening needs a fair amount of skill to pull off successfully because you've got to hold readers for an extended period before they get a real reason to continue reading.

'Once upon a time ...'

This is about beginning with backstory and exposition. Although the first stage in a conventional plot sequence is the exposition, this doesn't mean the actual text has to be exposition-style text with explanation and introductions. That's the old-fashioned way of doing things and why I call this the 'once upon a time' error.

> Once upon a time, there lived a widow woman and her
> son, Jack, on their small farm in the country.

That kind of text isn't terrible, it's just that it isn't a great
hook. In the olden days, people had more patience to sit and
wait for a story to develop. These days, we don't.

Compare these two opening lines from the made-up memoir
I gave earlier:

> I was born in 1932 in London and went to school in
> Camberwell.
>
> vs
>
> My world ended at 5:30 on a Tuesday morning in May,
> 1941.

The first opening line is classic exposition. It's the traditional but boring way of starting at the beginning and
explaining everything first. The second begins with the action
and makes a startling statement about the world ending.
Which opening line has the hook?

Once again, this isn't a hard-and-fast rule – if you know what
you're doing you can write a 'once upon a time' opening or any
of these other openings I've been so rude about. It all depends
on the effect you want to create. A writer who acts with skill and
purpose can get away with just about anything.

Are you feeling bereft because your opening lines have been
squashed? Here is a famous quote by a famous author that
should make you feel less alone:

> In writing, you must kill all your darlings. —*William
> Faulkner*

The context of this lesson

Your opening lines will sell your book. It's as simple as that. And yet most manuscripts by novice authors begin with random scenes and totally forgettable first lines. That's why this lesson is perhaps the most important of the whole book. If you don't grab them at hello, you've lost them. So be calculating and ruthless in choosing the right words. Surprise your readers and force them to take notice. Be a true storyteller, weaving words of magic that keep your readers entranced from the very first page.

Summary

Your first paragraph is the most important passage you'll write in your whole book:

- Open with a scene that presents a hook – a disrupting event that gives rise to questions in the mind of the reader or viewer.
- Open with first lines that immediately arouse curiosity and present a hook of their own. Ways of doing this include starting with a disruption, starting with a setting description that creates a sense of movement and foreboding, starting with dialogue, starting in the middle of the action (*in medias res*), and starting with a resonant statement that shocks the reader into paying attention.
- These principles apply to memoir and creative nonfiction as well.

Exercises

1. Brainstorm opening lines

Write at least three opening lines for possible stories. Don't think too hard about it – you're not going to actually write the stories, so give yourself the freedom to go wild. Try different ways of starting, for instance, with dialogue, in the midst of action, with description or with a startling statement.

If you get stuck, read through the examples of opening lines provided earlier in this chapter. Once your mind is tuned to good opening lines, they'll start popping into your mind spontaneously.

2. Write your opening lines

This is the last exercise in the course, so it's time to take a big step towards finishing the story you've been working on. For this exercise, choose your opening scene and craft an arresting first paragraph that hooks the reader and draws them into the story. If you've already written your opening, run the checklist of effective ways of starting a story and see if yours is as effective as it could be. If it doesn't contain a hook of some kind, rework it until it does. Here's a reminder of some good ways of crafting an effective opening:

- Start with a disruption – something happens that creates immediate questions in the reader's mind.
- Start with a setting description that creates a sense of movement and seduces with its delicious words, inviting the reader to step into another world.

- Start *in medias res.*
- Start with dialogue.
- Start with a startling, resonant statement that shocks the reader into paying attention.

Now over to you. Your opening lines:

CHAPTER 15

Conclusion and Class Project

Well done, you've reached the end of the programme! This course has promised that you will learn masterful fiction writing as you build your own story, so now it's time for you to put all the pieces together and complete your work-in-progress.

As you've progressed through the lessons, you will have come up with some story ideas, sketches and scenes. And you will have experimented with story structure and perhaps found ways to stitch some of those scenes into a rough draft of a short story. Or perhaps you've come up with an outline and a few scenes for a longer work. Whatever shape it has taken for you, I recommend you put everything together in one document and imagine you are submitting it as a class project. It's important that you put your work together like this so you get a sense of what you've achieved and offer your inner mind the reward of seeing a completed draft or collection of scenes. View this as your portfolio and your confirmation as being a real writer.

Before you sign off on your work, make sure you've incorporated what you've learned on this course. Check that your:

- Opening lines are arresting and create a hook
- Dialogue is authentic and well-punctuated
- Main characters are round and not just flat stereotypes
- Events, dialogue and narration are fuelled by some kind of conflict or desire (either inner or outer, subtle or overt)
- Narration uses 'showing' more than 'telling'
- Description is vivid and sensory (without over-describing)
- Point of view and tense are consistent within each sketch or scene

Naturally, not every piece or scene will exhibit all of these characteristics, so don't force anything. Just get a sense that all these elements are playing out somewhere in your writing.

All that remains is to say well done, you now have all the skills necessary to write publishable fiction that grabs the attention of readers as well as agents and publishers. You are already way ahead of most of the writers out there who are just winging it and hoping a masterpiece will magically emerge from their fingertips without any knowledge of the essential techniques of fiction. So grab your advantage and run with it. You might be surprised at what happens.

PART 4

The Writing Life

The first three parts of this book covered the technical nuts and bolts of writing publishable fiction. As with most pursuits, however, technical knowledge only gets you so far. To play the game fully, you also need to bring your heart and soul onto the field. So, in this final part, I'll address some of the mental and emotional aspects of the writing life. I'll also answer a few of the practical questions you'll probably have as you take your writing further and start wondering about things like editing and publishing.

CHAPTER 16

Your Writing Goals and Daily Practice

As you worked through the course in Parts 1 to 3 of this book you might have found yourself setting some writing goals for yourself. And if you didn't, then now is the time to do so. Concrete goals are the first step in bringing your creations from the world of ideas and inspiration into the real world. If you only write when you are inspired to write, then all you will have is a collection of story fragments and you will give up before anything worthwhile happens. But if you back up those calls of inspiration with a concrete plan of action and a timeframe for completion, you create a structure for more inspiration to flow.

So I invite you now to create some worthy writing goals for yourself. Don't get stuck by thinking that goals tie you down to an outcome that *has* to happen no matter what – goals are just formulations of intent that you will follow to the best of your ability, allowing the actual outcomes to take you in unexpected directions. Goals need to be adjusted as you start following them and discover more about what you really want. A goal is simply a way of starting the journey. So let's start.

Exercise: Goal setting

Take a moment to feel into the impulse and desire to write. What would you love to create? What would excite you and give your life meaning and fulfilment as you pursue it (for example, write a novel or screenplay, write a collection of short stories or personal essays, write a memoir)? Now write that down:

My goal:

....

....

Now break that big goal into manageable sub-goals, for instance:

- Completing a detailed plot outline.
- Writing the first rough draft of a novel, screenplay or memoir.
- Writing the first five stories of a collection.
- Write 10,000 words exploring different story ideas to see which one will work best.

You might be able to identify several sub-goals on the way to completing the major goal. Write these down.

My sub-goals:

....

....

And finally, imagine that you commit to working on this project every day, even if only for 45 minutes to an hour. How long do you think it might take to complete the first sub-goal? To estimate this, you might need to break your sub-goal down into rates of words per day or stories per month. If you commit to 500 usable words per day, then 10,000 words will take 20 days. It's also OK to just take a wild guess about how much time you'll need. The important thing is to set some kind of time deadline.

Completion date of first sub-goal (also note the required word rate or story/chapter rate per day, week or month to reach this goal):

Excellent work! You have your first writing goal and a commitment to achieving it by a certain date. Now the real work begins as you start a daily practice and make any necessary re-arrangements in your life to make space for this commitment.

Your daily writing practice

You've got an inspiring writing goal or two, and now you need to show up to your goals by dedicating regular time and effort to writing. For instance, you might decide you are going to write for one hour every morning, come hell or high water.

When you create this structure and stick to it (as far as possible), you will train your inner mind to show up for work at that particular time and give you the inspired words you are looking for. If you write only when you feel like it or 'when the spirit is with you', then you might find that nothing much happens at all. You need to create the structure, the vessel, for spirit to fill. You need to set the date and the time for your meeting with your creative angels, and then show up promptly (even if they don't).

I like to think of writing practice as a balance between two energies – the masculine and the feminine (or the yang and the yin). The masculine is about structure, discipline and authority – purposefully and sometimes fiercely defending the creative space and cutting out distractions. The masculine contains all the aspects over which you have some degree of control, including your will, your commitment, your craft and your boundaries. It also comes into play when you write very purposefully about something you already know, for example, a recipe or set of instructions. You already have the content and just need to express it.

The feminine, yin, is more about what you are not in control of – it's the state of receiving, as well as what is received. The yin of writing is when you step back and allow something else to appear. It's about going into what you don't know. It's the realm of pure inspiration where you are possessed by words and ideas that you did not consciously think up.

For me, the yang energy is about creating the vessel, while the yin energy fills it. Yang is about what you make, and yin is about what you are given. So if we apply it to our core practice of freewriting, yang energy gets you to sit down at the blank page and start putting words onto paper. This is the part you are in control of. But as you continue with the exercise you get more into a flow and yin energy begins to take over. You start getting unexpected insights and inspired lines that seem to come out of nowhere. You'll know you are in yin energy when it feels like you're just taking dictation – the words are appearing and you're not expending effort to create them.

To be an artist or writer you need to bring both energies into balance. If you are only into spirit and inspiration (yin) you will stay in the land of the unicorns and never come down to earth with a creation that entertains and transforms people. If you are only into discipline and structure (yang), you will never hear the music that comes from afar and your writing will remain dull and functional.

So now you have heard the call of desire to write (yin energy) and you have met this with some yang energy in the form of defining your first goals. The next step is to summon more yang energy to carve out the physical time and space into which you are going to invite the goddess/yin energy of the Muse.

Exercise: Creating the vessel

When are you going to write? Name the time of day, how much time, and what you might have to do to make this possible. (For example: *I will write one hour per day, in the morning before I go to work, and I will wake up earlier if necessary in order to do this. If I don't manage a morning session, I will do an evening session.*)

You now have a firm commitment to your goals and you will find that your writing output and power increase exponentially as you show up to your practice week after week. Do not make the mistake of showing up only when you feel like it. Some of your best writing will happen on days when you least feel like writing at all. When in doubt, do freewriting and just fill three pages with words. You might need to do this for several days if you are going through a particularly deep drought or are processing emotions and life events. At a certain point, you will break through and find the flow again.

And yes, you are allowed holidays from your daily practice now and then. If you feel you are getting stale and the writing is going nowhere, give yourself a break but set a date for returning to the work. As always, balance flexibility with structure and discipline.

CHAPTER 17

Getting Published

You've finished your novel, memoir or collection of stories – now what? Should you get the work edited and critiqued or start looking for a publisher? Or do you need an agent first? Or should you just bypass agents and traditional publishers and self-publish on Amazon?

Let's unpack these questions by looking at the general process you will follow once you've completed your writing and want to take the next steps.

1: Story checking and preparation

Contrary to popular belief, the first step after you have completed your manuscript is not to have it edited. If you are going the self-publishing route, editing is going to be your greatest expense, so you have to be absolutely sure that your story is ready for this investment. And if you want to find a traditional publisher, then you don't usually need a text editor as the publisher will take on this task.

What you need, first of all, is objective feedback on whether your story works. This means seeking out other authors or professionals who will critique your work. The no-cost option in this regard is to find what are known as beta readers – fellow writers who are willing to read the work and offer comment on it, usually in exchange for your comment on their work. If you join writers' groups on Facebook or in the real world you will often be able to find beta readers willing to offer constructive criticism of your writing. Many writers enjoy this role, so don't be afraid to put the offer out there.

If you have a budget to spend and want more substantive and professional feedback, you can get your work critiqued by a professional. Author coaches and many editors will offer this service. It can be pricey, but you will learn a lot from the feedback and it will be an investment in your growth as a writer.

Once you have implemented any feedback from your beta readers or professional critics, the next step is to do a self-edit to make sure the manuscript is as free of errors as possible. Use the built-in spelling checker in Microsoft Word or whichever writing software you are using to run a spell check on the document. Make sure to first set your language preference according to whether you are using US or UK spelling (generally, choose the spelling that will be used by the majority of your readers). Then run another check using an artificial intelligence writing checker like Grammarly or ProWritingAid. I have used Grammarly for years and seen the steady improvements in its capacity to understand sentences and suggest improvements. It will find errors that an ordinary spelling checker won't find. But be careful – not all its suggestions should be followed. It is early days for AI after all, and sometimes it just gets things wrong, so you need to ignore its suggestions when they're not on target.

Once you've done these checks and the manuscript is as publish-ready as you can get it, it's time to consider your publishing options.

2. Choosing a publishing model – traditional vs independent

Before Amazon, there was only one respectable way to get into print and that was by getting accepted by a mainstream publisher. Think of the big names like Penguin, Heinemann, HarperCollins, Macmillan and Simon & Schuster, plus smaller boutique or local publishers. The publisher would agree to publish your book and pay you royalties on books sold, typically around 10% of the cover price. They would take care of editing, cover design, production, marketing and getting your book into bookstores. In return, they would hold the copyright for the book for the period agreed to in your contract and would have creative control of the content. We now refer to this model as the traditional or mainstream publishing model. It's still an important pathway to publishing but it is no longer the only way.

The new model, which we can call independent publishing, was opened up by Amazon with its development of the Kindle and the e-reading market. Now, anyone can publish on Amazon and similar platforms with no or minimal setup costs. In the independent model, you have complete control of your book content and you don't have to spend months or years trying to find an agent who will represent your book. The barriers to entry are very low, which is good because it means you can publish just about anything you want, and a challenge because you'll be competing against millions of other titles, some of which are great and some of which are terrible. In the independent model, you have to pay for editing, layout and cover design and do all your own marketing, and you have to face the fact that your book will probably not sell in any great numbers without advertising. Now, this might not be a problem for you if you are writing a niche book that you don't expect to make money off, for example, a memoir that will be read mostly by family and friends. If you do choose to pursue profit from your book, be encouraged by the fact that you can earn substantially more in terms of royalties (up to 70% for ebooks and 50% for print) than with traditional publishing.

If you decide that you *do* want to make money with your books but you aren't up for the marketing and the expense of book preparation, then you should consider the traditional route. Traditional publishing also puts you in line for literary awards, makes you eligible for the bestseller lists like the New York Times list, and gets your books into the bookshops.

However, before progressing too far down this route, let's stop and take a reality check. Traditional publishing is now an extremely competitive place and the old way of authors sending in their manuscripts in the hope of being read are well and truly over, at least in the major markets of the English-speaking world. Now you have to jump through a number of hoops to get anywhere near a publisher. The first is that the major publishers never look at unsolicited manuscripts but rely on literary agents to do the filtering for them. This means you must first get an agent. And to get an agent, you need to prepare a book proposal or query letter in which you pitch your idea, present a sample of the text, and hope the agent will ask to see the rest of the manuscript. There are some finer details here that you can research but I'm just giving an outline so you know what the game involves. If you are fortunate enough to get an agent (which can take months) the agent will try to sell the work to a publisher, and that can take months or years.

But that's not all – mainstream publishers exist in a highly competitive world and the major ones are not interested in the small fry. They're only interested in books that will sell many thousands of copies. So if you don't yet have a big following on social media and you're not already well-known or controversial, then it's a bit more difficult to convince a publisher to invest in your work. Now, this isn't an absolute position and, of course, there are new writers with no following who get picked up by publishers, it's just that they have to have a damn fine book in their hands or they have to be writing in a trending or newsworthy topic. All of which means that, for most of us, landing a deal with a major publisher is a bit of a long shot and means playing a top-class game while being prepared for much waiting as various levels of the publishing food chain take their time considering the economic potential of our creations. In this light, going independent is a worthy and potentially profitable alternative. For some, it can even lead to a traditional publishing deal – the *Fifty Shades of Grey* series by E.L. James being a famous example of this. Basically, if you self-publish a few books and build good sales and a decent following, you will become more attractive to the big publishers and they might offer you a generous deal on your next book.

I'm not going to say anything more on the topic because to deal with it adequately would take a few more chapters, but I hope you now have at least some idea of the publishing landscape and a sense of which route you would like to pursue.

3. Getting your book edited

Once you've done your self-edit and you've decided on the publishing route you're going to take, it's time to consider editing. There are four levels of editing:

Editorial assessment

The editorial assessment is a high-level overview of your manuscript that provides feedback on whether the story works and where any problems might be lurking. It looks at plot, character arcs, pacing, style and any other big-picture elements of your work. The editorial assessment doesn't make any changes to your text. The output of the editorial assessment is a feedback report outlining the work's strengths, weaknesses and suggestions for improvements. Choose this level of edit if you want to make sure your story works or if you are having problems with the plot and need help figuring out how to fix it. Once you have implemented the recommendations of the assessment, you will still need to do a copy edit.

Developmental edit

A developmental edit is a more in-depth look at plot, character, pacing, style and other elements. Whereas an editorial assessment takes a very high-level view and gives a feedback report, the developmental edit starts working with the text and making changes or suggesting changes. Note that these changes are at the level of plot, characterisation, pacing and other story-level issues. It's not primarily about grammar, punctuation and spelling, though the editor might fix some of this or highlight particular issues for you to fix. This level of edit is ideal if you know your text has problems that an ordinary text edit (copy edit) won't be able to fix. The developmental editor will help you develop or build the text, which means they will refer some issues back to you for your attention. After a developmental edit, you will still need a copy edit.

Copy edit (line edit)

This is the edit that gets down to the nitty-gritty of your grammar, punctuation and spelling while also looking out for inconsistencies and tricky issues to do with point of view and tense. The copy editor is a language specialist and will make sure your sentence structure and expression are relatively error-free. This is an essential edit that most authors will need, though it is usually the most expensive edit as it takes the most time.

Proofreading

Proofreading is the final check before a book is published. It is usually done after a copy edit and focuses only on the typos and small issues that were missed in the copy edit. The proof edit is often done on paper printout, while all the other edits are performed in the electronic document. Proofreading usually costs less than copy editing because it involves less work. In traditional publishing, the publisher will give your book both a copy edit and a proof edit.

So which level of editing should you choose? If you are going to try the traditional publishing route, you usually don't need to get your book copy edited or proofread as most publishers will do this at their expense. However, to make sure your story works and is in a sellable state, you might want to consider investing in an editorial assessment or a developmental edit. View the cost of this exercise as an investment in your professional growth and in the success of your book.

If you are going the self-publishing route, you need a copy edit and sometimes also a developmental edit or an editorial assessment. No matter how good you are with language, you will simply not spot all the small errors that can cause readers to leave you a poor review. Copy editing is time-consuming work and will probably be your biggest expense in the publishing process. For a proper copy edit, you can expect to pay upwards of $1,200 for a book of 60,000 words (2021 rates). Now this can be a bit of a challenge for many indie authors, most of whom will take years to recoup their investment through book sales alone. So what often happens is that authors get the lowest level of editing possible, essentially just a proofread, and they find low-cost editors willing to do the job for cheap. You can find such editors on Fiverr and Upwork. I can't argue with the need to save costs, so I will just say that if you do have to go the low-cost route, make sure your text is already just about perfect before you send it to the editor/proofreader. Have at least one other person (a friend or a beta reader) give it a read-through first to find any errors. Also, don't expect the proofreader to correct all your grammar, spelling and punctuation errors – you are paying them to find the odd mistakes that you have missed. Your copy needs to be very clean already when you give it to them.

Note that readers of ebooks tend to be a bit more forgiving about small text errors than readers of print books. So if you are only publishing in ebook format, you can probably get away with a cheaper edit than if you are also publishing a print version.

If English is not your first language or you are not very fluent as a writer then I would recommend you do invest in a quality copy edit. The editor will put in the time to make your book publishable and help you avoid the poor reviews that will almost certainly sink your book before it goes anywhere at all.

CHAPTER 18

The Writer's Journey

The first novel I wrote was pretty darn good, possibly even brilliant. At least, that's what I thought when I sent the manuscript off to an agent. When I called the agent back after a month to get his verdict, it was quickly apparent that he was not particularly skilled in the art of offering an opinion. He told me quite bluntly that the story didn't work at all and that if I wanted to know what a masterpiece was I should read Don de Lillo's *Underworld*. He spent another minute or two extolling the virtues of this book, which he had clearly been reading at the time my miserable heap of words arrived on his desk. When I put the phone down, I made the firm decision to never write again, and then, as further punishment, went to the town library to find this mythical masterpiece which the agent had had so deftly wielded to crush my ego. A few weeks later, after finishing that tome of a book, I realised that I had indeed been in the presence of a master and the wisdom of my decision to never set pen to paper again was confirmed.

Fast-forward a year and I found myself writing again. This time, I thought, I'd get it right. Who gets their first novel published, anyway? Time to get back on the horse and do a better job. But after two years of labour, I realised that the story was rickety and going nowhere. I didn't need a crusty old agent to tell me that. With disappointment once again my companion, I closed the computer file and vowed never again to waste time with this writing lark. Time to focus on getting out of my lousy job and finally earn some good money.

And then, of course, I had an idea. It was brilliant, it consumed me day and night. The story poured forth from the heavens and commanded me to pick up the pen again and write. This time, yes *this* time, it would be different. I had learned my lesson, after all, and I decided that if this novel was going to go anywhere, I would need some help. So I enrolled in the Creative Writing Master's programme at the University of Cape Town and had the good fortune of being given South African literary great André Brink as my mentor. I couldn't believe my luck – André was a legend in my country, well-known for his prolific output and for being the first Afrikaans writer to have his work banned by the apartheid government. Naturally, I was in awe and intimidated as hell. Our first meeting, however, laid my fears to rest, as he turned out to be generous, down-to-earth and wonderfully supportive. Over the next two years we would meet every few months and he would comment on my latest work and offer advice where needed. When the novel was finished and he'd read the last chapter I cautiously asked him if he thought it was publishable, and he said it was indeed, and that he'd give me an intro to his own publisher. So much generosity in a mentor, it still makes me emotional just to remember it. To cut a long story short, the publisher looked at the manuscript and made an offer to publish. That novel, *Garden of the Plagues*, went on to win the Olive Schreiner award for debut fiction in South Africa and was shortlisted for the country's premier literary competition, the Sunday Times Literary Awards. At the awards dinner I was seated at a table with André, who had also been shortlisted. As the evening wore on, his wife, Karina, leaned over and said to me, "André and I are so hoping it will be you who wins." As it turned out, neither of us won, but André's generosity has stayed with me all these years as a reminder of all the qualities of a true mentor.

After that special year of being published and winning some critical acclaim, I was all set for the beginning of my great literary career. All I needed was the next novel. It should have been easy, right? But for some reason, nothing happened. Well, I did have an idea for a story but my draft was turned down by my publisher. I tried another and it went nowhere. For the next few years, I wrote on four or five novel ideas and not one of them was strong enough to go to completion. Instead, I was mired in the task of trying to make a living as a freelancer after having given up my day job to complete my novel, all the while burning with resentment at the fact that writing had let me down and left me in an extremely uncomfortable financial position. Weren't things supposed to work out if you followed your bliss? Clearly not, or perhaps I was just doing it wrong.

At this time I was teaching a semester course in creative writing at the University of Stellenbosch and I felt so disheartened by writing that I gave that up too. In retrospect, that was probably a mistake, because I was not seeing that life was offering me an opportunity to become more involved in teaching and mentoring writers. It was only much later, when some of my editing work naturally evolved into more of a coaching and story-critiquing role, that I was able to grasp the opportunity that was again being offered to me. This book is a response to that new impulse. When I first started mapping out the framework of this book I was still not deeply invested in the idea of teaching or supporting other writers, I simply wanted to present some technical knowledge that would help authors avoid the mistakes I had made in my own writing efforts and which I was seeing again and again in the work they submitted to me for editing. But as the writing progressed and I had to sharpen my writing skills to put all this down in words, I began to feel a renewed sense of purpose. I remembered what André Brink had given me and I felt inspired to pay it forward by embracing the role of mentor and coach to other writers. And as I began doing this, I felt my enthusiasm for writing fiction returning. Right now, I am being prodded by at least two story ideas that I am eager to start working on as soon as this book and the video course are done.

Which brings me to the point of this rather long story and why I'm sharing it with you, which is that it's important that you embrace the idea of writing being a journey. It's a true hero's quest full of highs and lows, setbacks, dark moments, sudden breakthroughs and startling epiphanies. You will meet allies and mentors along the way and you will need to reach deep for reserves of strength and creativity you did not know you had. In the end, you may produce just one proud work or you may become a prolific author with impressive sales figures, but ultimately, you are the work of art that is being created. Even if you are writing action-packed adventure stories or romances with no great psychological depth, the work of creating the writer-self who will get these stories down on paper can take considerable inner work. That is why I encourage you to think of yourself as being on a hero's journey where obstacles and failures are as much a part of the process as support and success. If you give up at the first challenge because the path feels less than blissful, then you are perhaps missing an opportunity to go deeper into your being to bring out the self that is worthy of the challenge.

You have been called to write because something deep within you wants to be expressed in the world. To bring forth this gift you will need to turn from the distractions of the ordinary world for a while and enter an unfamiliar territory with only your skill, your heart's desire and your intuition to guide you. All hero's journeys begin like this, with an ordinary man or woman who responds to a call and then leaves the security of the tribe to venture forth on paths unknown for a prize of great uncertainty. So if you have been called, and I would suggest that if you have read to these final words then indeed you have, then all that is left to say is be bold, find allies and mentors, and set out on your quest with a full heart and expectations of great adventure.

Connect with the Author

Russel Brownlee is an author, editor and creativity coach with a passion for writing and helping other writers follow their dream of being published and making a living with their art. Connect with him for author coaching, editorial assessments, and writing courses.

www.russelbrownlee.com

If you enjoyed this book and think it will be helpful for other writers, please leave a positive review on Amazon.